Modeling Mindsets

The Many Cultures of Learning From Data

Christoph Molnar

2023, First Edition

ISBN 9798358729339 (PAPERBACK)

Christoph Molnar
c/o MUCBOOK, Heidi Seibold
Elsenheimerstraße 48
80687 München, Germany

commit id: f9ada8d

Contents

Preface

Is a linear regression model statistical modeling or machine learning? This is a question that I have heard more than once, but it starts from the false premise that models somehow belong to one approach or the other. Rather, we should ask: What's the mindset of the modeler?

Differences in mindsets can be subtle yet substantial. It takes years to absorb a modeling mindset because, usually, the focus is on the methods and math rather than the mindset. Sometimes modelers aren't even aware of their modeling limitations due to their mindset. I studied statistics, which gave me an almost pure frequentist mindset. Because of that narrow lens on modeling, I often hit a wall in my modeling projects, ranging from a lack of causal reasoning to crappy predictive models. I couldn't solve these problems by doubling down on my current mindset. Instead, I made the most progress when I embraced new modeling mindsets. Modeling Mindsets is the book I wish I had read earlier to save myself time and headaches.

The inspiration for Modeling Mindsets was the article "Statistical Modeling: The Two Cultures" by the statistician Leo Breiman. His article was the first to show me that modeling is not only about math and methods but it's about the mindset through which you see the world. Leo Breiman's paper is over 21 years old and hasn't lost any of its relevance even today. Modeling Mindsets builds on the same principle of making mindsets explicit and embraces the multiplicity of mindsets. I kept Modeling Mindsets short, (mostly) math-free and poured over a decade of modeling experiences into it. My hope is that this book will still be relevant 21 years from now and a great investment for you.

Who This Book is For

This book is for everyone who builds models from data: data scientists, statisticians, machine learners, and quantitative researchers.

To get the most out of this book:

- You should already have experience with modeling and working with data.
- You should feel comfortable with **at least one of the mindsets** in this book.

Don't read this book if:

- You are completely new to working with data and models.
- You cling to the mindset you already know and aren't open to other mindsets.

You will get the most out of Modeling Mindsets if you keep an open mind. You have to challenge the rigid assumptions of the mindset that feels natural to you.

1 Introduction

Every day, people use data for prediction, automation, science, and making decisions. For example:

- Identifying patients prone to drug side effects.
- Finding out how climate change affects bee hives.
- Predicting which products will be out-of-stock.

Each data point has details to contribute:

- Patient with ID 124 got acne.
- Bee colony 27 shrank during the drought in 2018.
- On that one Tuesday, the flour was sold out.

Data alone aren't enough to solve the above tasks. Data are noisy and high-dimensional – most of the information will be irrelevant to the task. No matter how long a human analyzes the data, it's difficult to gain insights just by sheer human willpower.

Therefore, people rely on models to interpret and use data. A model simplifies and represents an aspect of the world. Models learned from data – the focus of this book – glue together the raw data and the world. With a model, the modeler can make predictions, learn about the world, test theories, make decisions and communicate results to others.

Models Have Variables And Learnable Functions

There is no philosophical consensus on the definition of a model. For our purpose, we'll go with this definition: **a**

mathematical model that consists of variables and functions.

Variables represent aspects of the data and the model:

- A numerical variable can contain the blood pressure of a patient.
- A 3-dimensional variable may represent the colors of a pixel.
- Variables can also represent abstract aspects like happiness.
- A cluster variable represents data grouping.

Variables have different names in different mindsets: Random variables, covariates, predictors, latent variables, features, targets, and outcomes. The names can reveal the role of a variable in a model: For example, the "target" or "dependent variable" is the variable the modeler wants to predict.

Functions relate the variables to each other (Weisberg 2012), see also Figure 1.1.

- A linear regression model expresses one variable as a weighted sum of the other variables.
- In deep Q-learning – a form of reinforcement learning – the value of an action (variable) is a function of the state of the environment (variables).
- A clustering model can be a function that takes, as input, the variables of the data point and returns its cluster (variable).
- The joint distribution of two variables describes the co-occurrence of certain variable values in terms of probability.
- A causal model represents the causal relationship between variables.

Functions range from simple, like $Y = 5 \cdot X$, to complex, like a deep neural network with millions of parameters.

So far, we have discussed variables and functions, the ingredients of a model, but not how they are connected to data. Modelers use data to find the best[1] function to relate the

---

[1]What the best model is depends on the mindset.

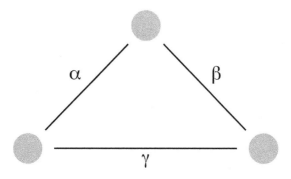

Figure 1.1: A mathematical model sets variables (dots) into relation (lines) using parameterized functions.

variables. Depending on the mindset of the modeler, the process of adapting a model's function is called estimation, training, fitting or learning. In this process, the model function is optimized using data:

- In a linear regression model, the coefficients (also called weights) are optimized to minimize the squared difference between the weighted sum and the target variable.
- K-means clustering cycles between assigning data points to cluster centers and optimizing the centers to minimize distances.
- A decision tree is grown by finding split points in variables using data.

Models Are Embedded In Mindsets

The interpretation and use of the model can't be derived from the model itself. Two mathematically identical models might be used in different ways by different modelers. The use of a model depends on the mindset.

A model is a mathematical construct that doesn't contain the purpose of the model. The purpose of the model – how to use and interpret it – depends on the modeling mindset. To derive knowledge about the world from the model, modelers need to make further assumptions.

Consider a linear regression model that predicts regional rice yield as a function of rainfall, temperature, and fertilizer use. It's a model, but interpretation needs a mindset:

- Can the modeler interpret the effect of fertilizer as causal to rice yield? *Yes, if based on a causal model.*
- Is the model good enough for predicting rice yields? *Depends if the modeler had a supervised learning mindset and has evaluated the generalization error properly.*
- Is the effect of fertilizer on yield significant? *This requires a frequentist mindset.*

A Mindset Is A Perspective Of The World

A modeling mindset provides the framework for modeling the world with data (Figure 1.2). Modeling means investigating a real-world phenomenon indirectly using a model (Weisberg 2007). Modeling mindsets are like different lenses. All lenses show us the world, but with a different focus. Some lenses magnify things that are close, and other lenses detect things that are far away. Also, some glasses are tinted so you can see in bright environments.

Mindsets differ in how they interpret probabilities – or whether probabilities are central to the mindset at all. While mindsets cover many different modeling tasks, they have some specific tasks where they really shine. Each mindset allows different questions. Hence, it shapes how to view the world through the model. In supervised machine learning, for example, everything becomes a prediction problem, while in Bayesian inference, the goal is to update beliefs about the world using probability theory.

A modeling mindset limits the questions that can be asked. Some tasks are out of scope because they don't make sense

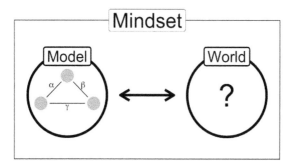

Figure 1.2: The real-world purpose of the model depends on the modeling mindset.

in a particular modeling mindset. Supervised machine learners formulate tasks as prediction problems. Questions about probability distributions are out of scope since the mindset is: to choose the model with the lowest generalization error given new data. So the best model could be any function, even an ensemble of many models (random forest, a neural network, linear regression model). If the best model can be any function, questions that a statistician would normally ask (hypothesis tests, parameter estimates) become irrelevant, as the modeler can't guarantee that the best model is a statistical model. Choosing a suboptimal model would violate the purely supervised learning mindset.

Each mindset has a different set of permissible models and ways to evaluate how good a model is. These sets may, however, overlap – for example, linear regression models are both used in frequentist inference and supervised learning. But whether the linear regression is a good model for a given task is evaluated in different ways, as we will discuss.

Mindsets Are Cultural

Modeling mindsets are not just theories; they shape communities and are shaped by people who apply the mindset. In many scientific communities, the frequentist mindset is very common. I once consulted a medical student for his doctoral thesis, and I helped him visualize some data. A few days later, he came back, "I need p-values with this visualization." His advisor had told him that any data visualization needed p-values. His advisor's advice was a bit extreme and not an advice that an experienced statistician would have given. However, it serves as a good example of how dominant a mindset can be and perpetuated by the community. Likewise, if you were trying to publish a machine learning model in a journal that publishes only Bayesian analysis, I would wish you good luck.

The people within a shared mindset also accept the assumptions of that mindset. These assumptions are usually not challenged but mutually agreed upon. At least implicitly. In a team of Bayesians, whether or not to use priors won't be challenged for every model. In machine learning competitions, the model with the lowest prediction error on new data wins. You will have a hard time arguing that your model should have won because it's the only causal model. Modelers that find causality important wouldn't participate in such a challenge. Only modelers that have accepted the supervised learning mindset will thrive in such machine learning competitions.

Mindsets Are Archetypes

The modeling mindsets, as I present them in this book, are archetypes: pure and extreme forms of these mindsets. In reality, the boundaries between mindsets are much more fluid:

- A data scientist who primarily builds machine learning models might also use regression models with hypothesis tests – without cross-validating the models' generalization error.
- A research community could accept analyses that use both frequentist and Bayesian models.

- A machine learning competition could include a human jury that awards additional points if the model is interpretable and causal.
- Ideas from one mindset might be applied in another: A modeler might use statistical models but evaluate them with the generalization error as typical in supervised learning.

Have you ever met anyone who is really into supervised learning? The first question they ask is, "Where are the labels?" The supervised machine learner turns every problem into a prediction problem. Or perhaps you've worked with a statistician who always wants to run hypothesis tests and regression models? Or have you had an intense discussion with a hardcore Bayesian about probability? Some people are walking archetypes of singular mindsets. But most people learned more than one mindset and embraced bits of other mindsets. Most people's mindset is already a mixture of multiple modeling mindsets, and that's a good thing. Having an open mind about modeling ultimately makes you a better modeler.

Mindsets Covered In This Book

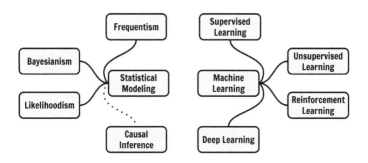

Figure 1.3: Overview of mindsets

- Statistical modeling and machine learning are "parent" mindsets.

- Frequentism, likelihoodism, and Bayesianism are flavors of statistical modeling.
- Supervised, unsupervised, reinforcement, and deep learning are flavors of machine learning.
- Causal inference can work with machine learning, but is culturally closer to statistical modeling.

For example, to understand Bayesian inference, you need to read the chapters on statistical modeling and Bayesianism.

The book is not exhaustive: some mindsets are *not covered*, although they are also data-driven. For example, the book doesn't cover mindsets based on sampling theory, experiments, or visualization. Also, some flavors such as self-supervised learning or non-parametric statistics didn't make it into this first edition of the book. If the book is popular, I'll write a second edition with more mindsets. Nevertheless, Modeling Mindsets already covers many of the most popular mindsets.

2 Statistical Modeling – Reason Under Uncertainty

Premise: The world is best approached through probability distributions.

Consequence: Estimate aspects of these distributions using statistical models to reason under uncertainty.

The statistician had come to duel the monster of randomness. The fight was fierce, and the statistician was driven back, step by step. But with every attack, the statistician learned more about the monster and suddenly realized how to win: figure out the data-generating process of the monster. With one final punch, the statistician separated signal from randomness.

Do you become more productive when you drink a lot of water? Your productivity will vary naturally from day to day – independent of hydration. This uncertainty obscures the effect of water intake on productivity. Uncertainty so often stands between data and clear answers.

Statistical modeling offers mathematical tools to handle uncertainty.[1] The rough idea is that the data are generated by a process that involves probability distributions or at least can be represented by distributions. Statistical models approximate the process by relating variables and specifying their distribution (in full or in part). The models are estimated with data, and modelers interpret them to reason under uncertainty.

---

[1] This chapter looks at the parts of statistical modeling that Bayesian inference, frequentist inference and likelihoodism share.

Every "Thing" Has A Distribution

Statistical modelers think in random variables. These variables are mathematical objects that encode uncertainty in the form of probability distributions. In statistical modeling, data are realizations of these variables (see Figure 2.1). Someone drinking 1.7 liters of water is a realization of the variable "daily water intake," but also a sign that this person might not be drinking enough. Other examples of variables:

- Outcome of a dice roll.
- Number of ducks in a park.
- Whether a customer canceled their contract last month.
- Daily number of duck attacks.
- The color of a t-shirt.
- Pain on a scale from 1 to 10 due to duck bites.

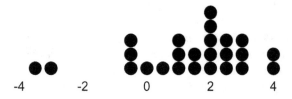

Figure 2.1: Each dot is a realization of a variable. The x-axis shows the variable's values. Dots are stacked by frequency

Probability distributions describe how variables behave. A distribution is a function that assigns a probability to each possible outcome of a variable. Value in, probability out. For the outcome of a fair dice, there are six possible outcomes, each with a probability of $1/6$. For continuous outcomes such as temperature, the Normal distribution is a common choice. See Figure 2.2 on the upper left.[2] Part of statistical modeling is to pick the best distributions that match the nature of the variables. Each distribution has parameters that modify it, such as mean or variance. That's an important property as it

---

[2]For continuous probability distributions the probability is given by an integral over a range of values.

allows fitting distributions to data. However, distributions alone aren't expressive enough for modeling – the modeler creates statistical models.

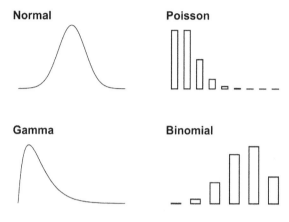

Figure 2.2: Distributions

Models Encode The Data-Generating Process

The modeler translates the data-generating process into a statistical model. All kinds of assumptions go into the model:

- Choice of relevant variables.
- How variables are distributed.
- If data are independent and identically distributed (IID).
- How variables are related to each other (such as linear, smooth effects, coding of categorical variables).

Let's say the modeler has data from an experiment where participants recorded both their daily water intake and the number of completed tasks. The modeler might assume that productivity, given water intake and day of the week, follows a Poisson distribution. More specifically, the modeler expresses the mean of the productivity distribution as a function of water intake and day of the week. Each participant appears multiple times in the data (multiple days), so the modeler makes assumptions that there is an additional "participant" effect that has to be accounted for. The modeler thinks through all these nuances of the data-generating process and encodes them in the statistical model.[3] This focus stands in contrast with machine learning, where solving the task at hand (like prediction) is more important than replicating the data-generating process.

You can see statistical models as having a fixed part, which are all these assumptions. In the next step, the model has to be combined with the data. That's where the flexible part of the model comes into play. Modelers "fit" models by adapting the parameters[4], such as regression coefficients, so that the data seem likely under the statistical model – aka having a high likelihood (see Figure 2.3). This fit is measured and optimized via the likelihood function, which takes as input the parameters and returns how likely the data are given these parameters. This makes model fitting an optimization problem (maximum likelihood estimation). While likelihoodists and frequentists directly maximize the likelihood function, Bayesians estimate the posterior parameter distribution, which is more complex than likelihood maximization alone.

There is another angle to model fitting: estimating parameters. Usually, the parameters within the model describe aspects of the distribution that the modeler is interested in. This can be a coefficient targeting the (conditional) mean, the correlation between variables, or even the full distribution.[5] In the productivity example, the modeler might be interested in the coefficients (parameters) that relate water intake and day of the week to the mean of the productivity distribution. The process of modeling can also be seen

---

[3] For the connoisseurs among you: The modeler might end up with something like a mixed-effects Poisson regression model.

[4] Statistical modeling has also distribution-free and non-parametric methods, which both relax some assumptions.

[5] Why not always model the full data distribution? Because it's complex or requires strong assumptions. Many questions can be answered with, for example, conditional distributions (like treatment effects).

as estimating model parameters such as these coefficients. Statistical modelers often draw conclusions via model parameters about real-world phenomena. Interpretation is often supported by element-wise representation (Freiesleben et al. 2022): All relevant parts of the data-generating process are represented within the model as variables, parameters or functions. Frequentists and Bayesians focus more on the estimation aspect, and likelihoodists focus more on the fitting aspect: likelihoodists compare models based on the likelihood ratio, which can tell which model fits better.

Figure 2.3: Fitting distributions to data

Good Models Satisfy Assumptions And Fit Data

The evaluation of statistical models consists of two parts: model diagnostics and goodness-of-fit evaluation.

The role of model diagnostics is to check whether the modeling assumptions are reasonable. This check is often visual: If a modeler assumes a variable follows a Normal distribution, they can check this assumption with a plot. Another assumption is homoscedasticity: The variance of the target is independent of other variables. Homoscedasticity can be checked with a residual plot, which shows on the x-axis the values of a variable and on the y-axis the residuals (actual target minus its predicted value) against each of the other variables. A Bayesian can verify with a posterior predictive check that the observed distribution of the target variable matches what the posterior distributions simulate.

A model that passes the diagnostic tests is not automatically a good model because it might not fit the data well enough. Statistical modelers use goodness-of-fit measures to compare different models and evaluate modeling choices, such as which variables to integrate into the model. The fit can be evaluated with goodness-of-fit measures bearing names such as R-squared, Akaikes Information Criterion, and the Bayes factor.

Goodness-of-fit is often computed with the same data used for fitting the statistical models. This choice may look like a minor detail, but it says a lot about the statistical modeling mindset.[6] The critical factor here is overfitting: The more flexible a model is, the more it might copy the randomness in the data. Many goodness-of-fit metrics, therefore, account for model complexity. In comparison, supervised learning relies on evaluation schemes that use unseen data to avoid overfitting and obtain honest estimates of the generalization error.

Models Enable Conclusions

Statistical models can help make decisions, understand the world, and make predictions. But using the model as a representation of the world isn't for free. The modeler must consider the representativeness of the data and make further (philosophical) assumptions.

Are the data representative of the population studied? Let's say modelers analyze data on whether a sepsis screening tool reduced the incidence of sepsis in a hospital. They concluded the tool reduced sepsis-related deaths at that hospital and want to make a recommendation to use it in all hospitals in the country. But are the data representative of all hospitals in the country? Or is there a reason why the patients of the

---

[6] A reminder that these mindsets are archetypes: some modelers only use statistical models but evaluate them with cross-validation as common in supervised learning.

studied hospital differ? A good modeler defines the population to be studied and discusses whether the data represent this population well.

When it comes to the modeler's attitude toward the nature of probability and what counts as evidence, the matter becomes philosophical:

> "It is unanimously agreed that statistics depends somehow on probability. But, as to what probability is and how it is connected with statistics, there has seldom been such complete disagreement and breakdown of communication since the Tower of Babel."

– Leonard Savage, 1972[7]

Different interpretations of probability and evidence lead to different flavors of the statistical modeling mindset:

- Frequentist inference sees probability as relative frequencies in the long run.
- Bayesian inference is based on an interpretation of probability as a degree of belief about the world.
- Likelihoodism equates the likelihood of a model as evidence for a hypothesis.

All these flavors of statistical modeling have a probabilistic view of the world in common.

Strengths & Limitations

+ Distributions and statistical models provide a language to describe the world and its uncertainties. The same language is even used to describe and understand machine learning algorithms under the label of statistical learning.

---

[7]Savage, Leonard J. The foundations of statistics. Courier Corporation, 1972.

+ Statistical modeling has an extensive theoretical foundation: From measurement theory as the basis of probability to thousands of papers for specific statistical models.

+ The data-generating process is a powerful mental model that encourages asking questions about the data.

+ Statistical models provide the means to reason under uncertainty, such as making decisions, understanding the world, evaluating hypotheses, and making predictions.

– Modeling the data-generating process can be quite manual and tedious, as many assumptions have to be made. More automatable mindsets, such as supervised learning, are more convenient.

– The statistical modeling mindset struggles with complex distributions, like image and text data. This is where machine learning and especially deep learning shine.

– Goodness-of-fit doesn't guarantee high predictive performance on new data. If the goal is to make predictions, a supervised learning approach is more suitable.

3 Frequentism – Infer "True" Parameters

Premise: The world is best approached through probability distributions with fixed but unknown parameters.

Consequence: Estimate and interpret the parameters using long-run frequencies to make decisions under uncertainty.

Once upon a time, there was a frequentist who dealt with p-values. She was the best in the business, and people would flock to her from all over to get their hands on her wares. One day, a young scientist came to the frequentist's shop. The scientist said: "I'm looking for the p-value that will allow me to get my paper published." The frequentist smiled and reached under the counter. She pulled out a dusty old book and thumbed through the pages until she found what she was looking for. "The p-value you're looking for is 0.05," she said. The scientist's eyes lit up. "That's exactly what I need! How much will it cost me?" The frequentist leaned in close and whispered, "It will cost your soul."

Drinking alcohol is associated with a 1.81 higher risk of diabetes in middle-aged men. At least, this is what a study claims (Kao et al. 2001). The researchers modeled type II diabetes as a function of variables such as alcohol intake. The researchers used frequentist inference to draw this conclusion from the data. There is no particular reason why I chose this study other than it's a typical frequentist analysis. Modelers[1] that think in significance levels, p-values, hypothesis tests, and confidence intervals are likely frequentists.

---

[1] Why I am not using the term "statistician" here: Statisticians do more than just statistical modeling. They visualize data, plan experiments, collect data, complain about machine learning, design surveys, and much more.

In many scientific fields, such as medicine and psychology, frequentist inference is the dominant modeling mindset. Frequentist papers follow similar patterns, make similar assumptions, and contain similar tables and figures. Understanding frequentist concepts such as confidence intervals and hypothesis tests is, therefore, one of the keys to understanding scientific progress. Frequentism has a firm foothold in the industry as well: Statisticians, data scientists, and whatever the future name of the role will be, often use frequentist inference, from analyzing A/B tests for a website to calculating portfolio risk to monitoring quality on production lines.

Probability Is A Long-Run Frequency

Frequentist inference is a statistical modeling mindset relying on variables, distributions, and statistical models. But it comes with a specific interpretation of probability: Probability is seen as the relative frequency of an event in infinitely repeated trials. But how do these long-run frequencies help gain insights from the model?

Let's go back to the 1.81 increase in diabetes risk among men who drink a lot of alcohol. 1.81 is larger than 1, so there seems to be a difference between men who drink alcohol and the ones who don't. But how can the researchers be sure that the 1.81 is not a random result? If you flip a coin 100 times, and it comes up with tails 51 times, our gut-feeling would say that the coin is fair. But where is the threshold? Is it 55 tails? 60? Viewing probability as long-run frequencies allows the modeler to define a threshold to decide when the coin is unfair. In addition, frequentists assume that each parameter has a fixed, true value. Repeated observations reveal the true values in the long run. The coin has a fixed probability for tails, and the modeling goal is to estimate (=uncover) it and quantify how certain the estimate is.

The researchers of the study applied the same type of frequentist thinking to decide whether the effect of alcohol is random or not. In this study, the parameter of interest was a

Figure 3.1: The line shows how the relative frequency of tails changes as the number of coin tosses increases from 1 to 100 (left to right).

coefficient in a logistic regression model. The diabetes study reported a 95% confidence interval for the alcohol coefficient ranging from 1.14 to 2.92. The interval doesn't contain 1, so the researchers concluded that alcohol is significantly associated with diabetes in men. We will discuss confidence intervals in more detail later in this chapter, as they are typically frequentist.

Imagined Experiments Underpin Inference

The best way to understand frequentism is to slowly work our way from the data and statistical model to the estimator to imagined experiments and finally to a decision.

1) Data Are Random Variables

Assume a modeler has observed 10 independent draws of a variable. Let's say we are talking about the weights of 10 apples. The modeler first assumes a statistical model for the weight variable by saying that it follows a Gaussian distribution. The modeler wants to know A) the average weight of an apple, including uncertainty estimates, and B) whether the average apple weighs less than 90 grams.

2) Estimators Are Random Variables

To answer the questions, the modeler first estimates the mean of the apple weight distribution. The estimation, in this case, is simple: add all observed values and divide by 10. Let's say the result is 79 grams. As a function of a variable, this mean estimator is a random variable itself. And the estimated mean of 79 is just one observation of that variable. The mean estimator is a rather simple estimation for a simple statistical model. We can imagine more complex models for the apples:

- A statistical model that relates the weight of an apple with its "redness".
- The weight distribution might be estimated conditional on variables such as apple type and season.
- Another model might target the 90% quantile of apple weights.

3) Long-Run Frequencies Interpretation

79 is smaller than 90 (question B). But the estimator is a random variable that comes with uncertainty. Assuming that the true average weight is 90, couldn't a sample of 10 apples weigh 79 grams on average, just by chance?

Bad news: The modeler has only one observation of the mean estimate and no motivation to buy more apples. Who on earth should eat all those apples? Good news: The modeler can derive the distribution of the mean estimate from the data distribution. Since the apple weights follow a Gaussian distribution, the modeler concludes that the mean follows a t-distribution.[2] The distribution of the mean has to be interpreted in terms of long-run frequency: It tells the modeler what to expect of the mean estimates in future experiments. Now the modeler has an estimate of the average weight of the apple and even knows the distribution, which is enough

---

[2]The average of a Gaussian distributed variable also follows a Gaussian distribution. However, if the variance is unknown and is estimated from data, the average follows a Student's t-distribution.

to quantify the uncertainty of the estimator. The modeler could visualize the distribution of the mean estimate, which would help with question A) about uncertainty. The modeler might also eyeball whether 90 grams seems likely (question B). But that's not good enough for the frequentist.

4) Making Decision Based On Imaginary Experiments

To draw conclusions about the population, the frequentist elaborates on how the mean estimate would behave if the experiment were repeated. The experiment was: Sample 10 apples, weigh them, and calculate the average weight. The frequentist has two tools available to make probabilistic statements about the average weight of the apples. One tool is hypothesis tests, and the other is confidence intervals. Both tools make clear, binary statements about which values are likely and which are not, allowing clear-cut decisions.

Decide With Tests And Intervals

A **hypothesis test** is a method to decide whether the data support a hypothesis. In the apple case: Does the observed average of 79 grams still support the hypothesis of 90 grams average apple weight? Ninety grams is also called the null hypothesis. Based on the assumed distributions, the corresponding test would be a one-sample, one-sided Student t-test. The t-test calculates a p-value that indicates how likely a result of 79 (or more extreme) is if 90 grams is the true average apple weight. If the p-value is below a certain confidence level (often 5%), then 79 is so far away from 90 that the modeler rejects the 90-gram-hypothesis. If the null hypothesis is really true, the test would falsely reject the hypothesis in 5% of the cases (1 out of 20). This so-called null hypothesis significance testing [3] is popular but also criticized for being simplistic and resulting in many false positive findings due to p-hacking (Head et al. 2015) and multiple testing.

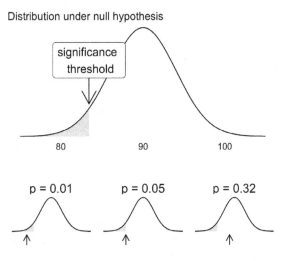

Figure 3.2: Frequentists can make binary decisions based on hypothesis tests. If the observed estimate is too extreme (grey area) under the assumed distribution of the null hypothesis, the null hypothesis is rejected.

Confidence intervals are an alternative. Hypothesis tests and confidence intervals ultimately lead to the same decisions, but confidence intervals are more informative. These intervals quantify how certain the estimate was: the narrower the interval, the more certain the estimate. The confidence interval is the region that likely covers the true parameter, which is assumed to be fixed but unknown. But it would be wrong to say: There is a 95% chance that the true parameter falls into this interval. A big No-No. If the modeler wants this type of interpretation, they better knock on the

---

[3]There are two "main" approaches for hypothesis testing: The Fisher approach, and the Neyman-Pearson approach. Null hypothesis significance testing is a combination of the two (Perezgonzalez 2015).

Bayesians' door. But for the frequentist, the experiment is done. Either the parameter is in the resulting interval, or it isn't. Instead, the frequentist interprets the 95% confidence interval in terms of long-run frequencies: If the modeler repeated the experiment many times, 95% of the time, the corresponding confidence interval would cover the true parameter. A repetition of the experiment means: draw another ten apples and compute confidence intervals from this new sample.[4] This sounds like nitpicking, but understanding this difference makes it easier to understand Bayesian inference.

Strengths & Limitations

+ Frequentist inference enables decisions. This simplicity is one of the reasons why frequentism is popular for both scientific publications and business decisions.

+ Once you understand frequentist inference, you can understand the analysis section of many research articles.

+ Frequentist methods are fast to compute, often faster than methods from Bayesian inference or machine learning.

+ Compared to Bayesianism, no prior information about the parameters is required.

– Frequentism incentivizes modelers to **over-simplify questions** into yes-or-no questions.

– The focus on p-values encourages **p-hacking**: the search for significant results to get a scientific paper published. P-hacking leads to many false findings in research.

---

[4]When frequentists propose estimators for confidence intervals, they actually have to conduct the "imagined" experiments. To quantify the coverage of the interval, the frequentists repeats the simulated experiment thousands of times.

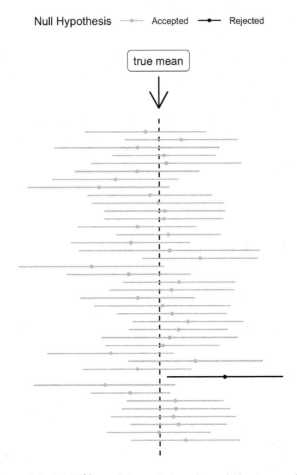

Figure 3.3: 20 95% confidence intervals and the true value.

– The frequentist interpretation of probability can be awkward, especially for confidence intervals. Bayesian credibility intervals seem to have a more "natural" interpretation of uncertainty.

– Frequentist analysis depends not only on the data but also on the experimental design. This is a violation of the likelihood principle. See the Likelihoodism chapter.

4 Bayesianism – Update Parameter Distributions

Premise: The world is best approached through probability distributions with probabilistic parameters.

Consequence: Update the prior parameter distributions using data to obtain the posterior distribution and draw conclusions.

A Bayesian walks into a bar and asks for a beer. The bartender says, "You're not allowed to drink here." The Bayesian looks around and sees that there are no other customers, so she asks, "Why not? Is it because I'm a Bayesian?" The bartender replies, "Yes, we don't allow Bayesians in here." The Bayesian is about to leave, but then she asks "What would happen if I came in here and told you that I'm not a Bayesian?" The bartender would reply, "That's impossible. Everyone is a Bayesian."

People teaching Bayesian statistics usually start with Bayes' theorem. Or, for a more philosophical twist, they start with the Bayesian interpretation of probability as degree of belief. But there is one Bayesian premise, from which the entire Bayesian mindset unfolds: **Model parameters are random variables.**

The mean of a distribution, the coefficient in a logistic regression model and the correlation coefficient – all these parameters are variables and have a distribution.

Let's follow the implications of the parameters-are-variables premise to its full conclusion:

- Parameters are variables.

- Therefore, the modeling goal has to be the parameter distribution given the data.
- But there is a problem. It's unclear how parameters *given* data are distributed. The distribution of data given parameters is more natural to estimate.
- Fortunately, a mathematical "trick" helps: Bayes' theorem.
- The theorem inverses the condition to P(data | parameters), which is the good old likelihood function.
- Bayes' theorem also involves P(parameters), the priori distribution.
- That's why Bayesians must specify a parameter distribution *before* observing data.
- Model estimation equals update from priori to posterior.
- Bayes' theorem also involves the term $P(X)$ called the evidence, which is usually unfeasible to estimate.
- This makes Bayesian models a bit more computationally intense to estimate.

Let's go deeper, and this time we start with Bayes' theorem. Using Bayes' theorem, the posterior is: posterior = (likelihood x prior) / evidence (Figure 4.1).

Figure 4.1: The posterior distribution (right) is the scaled product of prior and likelihood.

The priori is the probability distribution of the parameter before taking any data into account. The priori is "updated" by multiplying it by the data likelihood and dividing it by the evidence. The result is the posterior probability distribution, an updated belief about the parameters.

Bayes Demands A Prior

Bayesians assume that parameters have a prior probability distribution. Priors are a consequence of saying that parameters are random variables and a technical requirement for working with Bayes' theorem.

But how can Bayesians know the distribution of parameters *before* observing any data? Like, what's the prior distribution of a parameter in logistic regression that models the effect of alcohol on diabetes? Many considerations go into the choice of a prior.

The first consideration in choosing a prior is the parameter space, which is the set or range of values that the parameters can take on. For example, can the parameter only take on positive values? Then the prior must have a probability of zero for negative values, for example, the Gamma distribution.

The Bayesian can encode further domain knowledge with the prior. If the data follow a Binomial distribution (say, the number of tails in coin tosses), the Beta distribution is a possible prior for the success probability parameter (see Figure 4.2). The Beta distribution itself has parameters through which the modeler can instill further domain knowledge. Maybe there is reason to expect the parameter to be symmetrically distributed around 0.5, with 0 and 1 being rather unlikely. This would make sense for coin tosses. Or maybe the parameter is lower, around 0.25? There is even a Beta prior that puts the greatest probability symmetrically on 0 and 1.

Without domain knowledge about the parameter, the modeler can use "uninformative" or "objective" priors (Yang and Berger 1996). Uninformative priors may produce results identical or similar to those of frequentist inference. However, objective priors are not always as objective as they might seem and are not always easy to come by.

Another factor influencing the choice of prior is mathematical convenience: Conjugate priors remain in the same family of distributions when multiplied by the right likelihood functions, allowing the derivation of the posterior distribution analytically – a big plus before improvements in computational resources shook up the Bayesian landscape.

Critics of the Bayesian mindset decry that the choice of a prior is subjective. Bayesians might also be annoyed having to pick priors, especially if the model has many parameters and the prior choice is not obvious. But while priors can be seen as a problem, they can also be a solution:

- Priors can regularize the model, especially if data are scarce.
- Priors can encode domain knowledge and prior experimental results.
- Priors allow a natural handling of measurement errors and missing data.

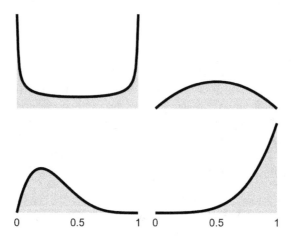

Figure 4.2: Various Beta prior distributions for the success probability in a Binomial distribution.

Fun fact: Bayesian models can, in theory, already be used, for example for making predictions.[1] But of course, the goal is to learn from data, so the prior is updated using the likelihood.

---

[1]This is called the prior predictive simulation and it's used to check whether the chosen priors produce reasonable data.

The Likelihood Unites All Statistical Mindsets

Prior aside, Bayesians make assumptions about the data distribution to specify the likelihood function P(data | parameters) just like frequentists and likelihoodists. Discussions often focus on the differences between the mindsets, but at the core, the three mindsets all use the likelihood. Especially in cases with a lot of data, models from different statistical mindsets will result in similar conclusions. However, comparisons often focus on the use of priors or other differences. The more data, the more certain the likelihood becomes and the impact of the prior vanishes.

While frequentists and likelihoodists get their inference mostly from the likelihood function, Bayesians want the posterior.

The Posterior Is The Modeling Target

The goal of the Bayesian modelers is to estimate the posterior distributions of the parameters. Once the modelers have the posteriors, they can interpret them, make predictions, and draw conclusions about the world.

In the ideal case, the posterior can be written down as an explicit formula and computed directly. But for most Bayesian models, it's impossible to obtain a closed form of the posterior. The problem is the evidence term in the Bayes' theorem: it's usually unfeasible to compute.

Fortunately, Bayesians have a way out: Instead of computing the posterior, they sample from it. Approaches such as Markov Chain Monte Carlo (MCMC) and derivations thereof are used to generate samples from the posterior distribution. The intuition behind this procedure: MCMC is producing random walks through the posterior, "visiting" regions with a large posterior proportionally more often. That's why samples can be seen as samples from the posterior. While this

sampling sounds tedious, most Bayesian modeling software
runs MCMC automatically. But it can be slow, especially
compared to frequentist maximum likelihood procedures. A
quicker but heuristic alternative is variational inference (Blei
et al. 2017).

The posterior distributions contain everything that the models learned from the data. Visualizing the posteriors provides
access to that full information. But people are fans of numbers and tables as well: the fewer and simpler, the better.
While some argue not to summarize the posterior (Tiao and
Box 1973), many modelers do it anyways to simplify results.
Any method that describes distributions can be used. Some
examples:

- The parameter value with the highest posterior probability (MAP).
- Probability that the parameter is >10.
- 95% credible interval that ranges from the 2.5% to the
  97.5% quantile.

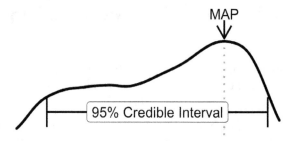

Figure 4.3: Describing the posterior distribution with the
          95% credibility interval and the maximum a pos-
          teriori estimation (MAP).

Use The Posterior To Learn About The World

Like in the other statistical modeling mindsets, Bayesians
build statistical models to approximate the data-generating

process with distributions. Learning from data means updating model parameters. But after the update, there is no point estimate of the parameters. Instead, the modeler gets a complete distribution, including uncertainty. But the posterior doesn't encode uncertainty inherent in nature, as in quantum mechanics. Instead, the posterior expresses the uncertainty of **information about the parameters**. That's different from how frequentists connect their statistical models to the world. Frequentists assume there are some unknown but fixed parameters that can be approximated with statistical models. Uncertainty is a function of the estimators, and conclusions about the world are derived from how these estimators are expected to behave when samples and experiments are repeated.

Another consequence of parameters being random variables: To predict, the Bayesian must simulate. Because if parameters are random variables, so are the predictions. Prediction with a Bayesian model means: sample parameters from the posteriors, then make predictions with the model. Repeat that multiple times and get a distribution of the prediction. The uncertainty of the parameters propagates into the uncertainty of predictions. If that seems inconvenient at first glance, it's much more honest and informative than a point estimate at a second glance. Uncertainty is a natural part of Bayesian modeling.

Strengths & Limitations

+ Bayesian models can leverage prior information, such as domain knowledge.

+ Bayesian inference provides an expressive language to build models that naturally propagate uncertainty. This makes it easy to work with hierarchical data, measurement errors and missing data.

+ The Bayesian interpretation of probability can be more intuitive than frequentist interpretation: When practitioners misinterpret frequentist confidence intervals, it's often because they interpret them as credible intervals.

+ Bayesian inference decouples inference (estimate posterior) and decision making (draw conclusions from posterior). Frequentist hypothesis tests entangle inference and decision-making.

– Choosing a prior can be difficult and be criticized as subjective.

– Bayesian methods are mathematically demanding and computationally expensive.

– When used exclusively for decisions, all the additional information about the entire posterior may appear as unnecessary overhead.

5 Likelihoodism – Likelihood As Evidence

Premise: The world is best approached through probability distributions and likelihoods.

Consequence: Use the likelihood of statistical models as evidence and to compare hypotheses.

A frequentist, a Bayesian, and a likelihoodist walk into a wine bar. A sommelier quickly joins the three. The Bayesian wants to hear the sommelier's opinion of the wines. The frequentist asks about the process: is the number of wines fixed, or does it stop with the first suitable wine? The likelihoodist ignores the sommelier and starts tasting the wines.

Frequentist inference has a long list of limitations. But it's still the dominant statistical mindset in science and elsewhere. Bayesian analysis has seen a resurgence thanks to increased computational power for sampling from posteriors with MCMC. But using subjective prior probabilities doesn't sit well with many statisticians. Could there be another way to "reform" the frequentist mindset? A mindset without the flawed hypothesis testing and without priors?

Likelihoodism is the purist among the statistical modeling mindsets: it fully embraces the likelihood function as evidence for a statistical hypothesis. Likelihoodism is an attempt to make statistics as objective as possible. It's also impractical, as we will see. Nonetheless, the likelihoodist mindset offers a fresh perspective on Bayesian and frequentist inference and an interesting approach to comparing hypotheses.

Statistical Mindsets Use Likelihood Differently

The likelihood function links observed data to theoretic distributions.

- Bayesians multiply prior distributions with the likelihood to obtain posterior distributions of the parameters.
- Frequentists use the likelihood to estimate parameters and construct "imagined" experiments that teach us about long-run frequencies (hypothesis tests and confidence intervals).
- Likelihoodists view the likelihood as evidence derived from data for a statistical hypothesis.

Likelihoodists are likelihood-purists and therefore reject the non-likelihood elements from frequentism and Bayesianism: They reject priors because they are subjective; They reject the frequentists' reliance on "imagined" experiments because these never-observed experiments violate the likelihood principle.

Let's take a look at the likelihood principle that is so central to the likelihoodist mindset.

Get Rid Of Priors And Imagined Experiments

"The likelihood principle asserts that two observations that generate identical likelihood functions are equivalent as evidence." (Richard 2017) As a consequence, all evidence that comes from the data about a quantity of interest, such as a model parameter, has to be part of the likelihood function. If we reverse the statement: The likelihood principle is violated if any information from the data enters the analysis outside of the likelihood. Both the Bayesian and the likelihoodist approaches adhere to the likelihood principle: All evidence from the data about the parameters is included in the likelihood. Bayesians use priors, but as long as they don't include any information from the data, it's fine. [1]

Frequentists use hypothesis tests, confidence intervals and p-values. All of these require "imagined" experiments, including an assumption of how these would be distributed.

Suppose a frequentist wants to see whether a coin is fair or if the head comes up more often. The null hypothesis says that the coin is fair, and the alternative hypothesis says that the coin produces more head tosses. The experiment has two variables: the number of heads and the number of coin tosses. Imagine two experiments that produce the same data:

1. Flip the coin 12 times. Observe 9 heads.
2. Flip the coin until the tail appears 3 times. The third tail appears on the 12th flip.

Same outcome but different stopping criteria. Should both experiments come to the same conclusion about the fairness of the coin? Depends on the mindset.

- Both experiments have the same likelihood, up to a constant factor. Likelihoodists would say that both experiments carry the same evidence.
- Frequentists might use a hypothesis test with a confidence level of 5%. Since the experiments have different stopping criteria, the frequentist uses different tests. As a result, the frequentist would reject the null hypothesis in experiment 2), but would not reject it in experiment 1).

I'll spare you the math behind this example.[2] The coin flip scenario is not completely artificial: Imagine a domain expert asks a statistician to perform an analysis with 1000 data points. For the frequentist, it matters whether the domain expert had a rule to stop after 1000 data points or whether the expert would continue collecting data depending on the outcome of the analysis.

---

[1] The likelihood principle is violated when data is used to inform the prior. For example, empirical priors violate the likelihood principle.

[2] https://en.wikipedia.org/wiki/Likelihood_principle

For the likelihoodist, the stopping criterion doesn't matter because of the likelihood principle. But the likelihood principle alone isn't sufficient to create a coherent modeling mindset, as it doesn't offer guidance on how to evaluate models. That's what the law of likelihood is for.

Compare Hypotheses Using Likelihoods

The law of likelihood allows the modeler to use the likelihood as evidence for a hypothesis. The law says (Hacking 1965):

If the likelihood for hypothesis A is larger than for hypothesis B, given some data, then the data counts as evidence that supports A over B, and the ratio of the likelihoods measures the strength of this evidence. Hypotheses A and B can be the same regression model, except that model B uses an additional variable. For example, model A predicts diabetes from diet, and model B predicts from diet and age. Both models produce a likelihood score, which the modeler can compare. Thanks to the law of likelihood, the modeler may interpret the ratio of likelihoods as evidence.

Likelihoodists may use a rule of thumb for judging the strength of evidence. For example, a likelihood ratio of eight is considered "fairly strong" and 32 or more is considered "strong favoring" (Richard 2017).

Likelihoodists also use the likelihood ratio for describing the uncertainty of parameter estimates using likelihood ratio intervals: a range of parameter values where the likelihood ratio remains below a specified threshold, compared to the estimate (see Figure 5.1).

The law of likelihood is stronger than the likelihood principle: The likelihood principle states that all evidence from the data must be in the likelihood; The law of likelihood describes how evidence can be quantified and compared.

The idea of likelihood ratios also lives in other statistical modeling mindsets. In frequentism, likelihood ratios are often used as test statistics for hypothesis tests. Likelihood

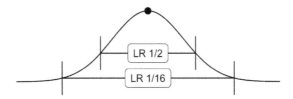

Figure 5.1: 1/2 and 1/16 likelihood ratio intervals.

ratio tests are typically used for nested models, where the variables of the first model are a subset of variables of the second model. Bayesians may use the Bayes factor to compare the ratio of two posteriors. If both models use the same priors, this ratio is the likelihood ratio.

But the likelihood ratio has a big problem. While a likelihoodist may interpret it as evidential favoring, the mindset lacks a mechanism to provide a definitive answer. Frequentists can use tests to decide on one hypothesis or the other. But testing is not allowed for the likelihoodist, or otherwise, they would violate the likelihood principle. The likelihood ratio is only an estimate and has some estimation error. How does the modeler know that a ratio of three is not just noise and that with a fresh data sample, it would be 0.9? Attempts to find a cut-off lead to frequentist ideas (which are rejected). Likelihoodism also rejects the idea of Bayesian model interpretation. Bayesian inference estimates posterior probabilities, which may be interpreted as updated beliefs about the parameter values and conclusions may be drawn from them. Likelihoodism doesn't provide the same type of guidance.

Strengths & Limitations

+ Likelihoodism is a coherent modeling approach: all information is contained in the likelihood. Frequentism, in contrast, is more fragmented, with long lists of differently motivated statistical tests and confidence intervals.

+ Likelihoodist inference adheres to the likelihood principle.

+ Likelihoodist ideas also have a home in Bayesian and frequentist modeling.

– Likelihoodism doesn't provide guidance in the form of belief or decision. Evidence is less practical.

– To be more specific: There is no good mechanism for deciding if there is enough evidence for one hypothesis.

– Likelihoodism allows only relative statements. It can't state the probability that a statistical hypothesis is true – only how its evidence compares to another hypothesis.

6 Causal Inference – Identify And Estimate Causes

Premise: The world is best approached through causal reasoning.

Consequence: Identify the underlying causal model and estimate the causal effects using statistical models or machine learning.

Once upon a time, a king asked his royal statisticians, "Are my subjects unhappy?" The statisticians consulted their data and concluded, "About 20% are unhappy, Your Majesty." The king pondered. "Ponies", he finally said, "Do my unhappy subjects have ponies?" "No, Your Majesty, the unhappy subjects don't have ponies." "Then give them ponies." The statisticians were alarmed. "Your Majesty, we can't give them ponies and expect them to be happy. It's only a statistical association." The king was displeased. "Ponies," he repeated, "give them ponies!" The next day, the unhappy subjects woke up to find ponies in their yards. They were overjoyed! The statisticians were stunned. "Your Majesty, the ponies are working!" "Of course they are," said the king. "Everyone knows that ponies cause happiness."

Some time ago, I worked with a rheumatologist on axial spondyloarthritis, a chronic condition associated with inflammation of the spine. Does a type of drug, TNF-alpha blockers, reduce problematic bone formation in the spine (ossification)? Infusion or injection of the blockers is great for reducing inflammation. Therefore, it would be unethical to withhold the drugs in a clinical trial. The next best option for

studying the drug effect on ossification: a statistical model
with observational data. To predict ossification, the model
included several variables such as patient age, disease duration, inflammation levels, medication, etc. The intermediate
analysis showed that the drug didn't reduce ossification.

By coincidence, the senior statistician of the patient registry
attended a course on causal inference at about the same time.
Applying what she had learned, she identified a flaw in the
model: Inflammation was a potential mediator of the effect
of TNF-alpha blockers on long-term ossification (see 6.1).

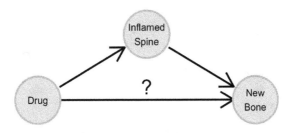

Figure 6.1: The drug was known to influence (reduce) inflammation. Inflammation was thought to cause ossification (new bone formation). The drug can, in
theory, reduce ossification in two ways: directly,
or indirectly via reducing inflammation.

The effect of the drug can be divided into direct and indirect effects. The total effect is the direct effect of the drug
plus any indirect effects, and in this case, via reducing inflammation. We were interested in the total effect of the
drug, but how we had specified the model, the coefficient
for the drug had to be interpreted as a direct effect. The
indirect effect was fully reflected by the coefficient for the
inflammation level (measured after the start of medication).
We therefore removed the inflammation variable[1] and did a

---

[1] Doesn't inflammation confound the relation between decision to treat
and ossification? Or is it a mediator? It depends on the time of the
measurement. In the faulty model, inflammation was considered
after treatment started, making it a mediator of the drug. Later,
we adjusted the model to include inflammation measured before
treatment start, making it a confounder.

mediator analysis. After removal, the coefficient for the drug could be interpreted as a total effect. The model then clearly showed that TNF-alpha blockers reduce ossification via reducing inflammation levels (Molnar et al. 2018). It feels like common sense to me in hindsight, but I didn't have a causal inference mindset at the time.

Causality Is Often Ignored

I guess we all have an intuition about causality. Rain is a cause of a wet lawn. A drug can be a cause of cure. An environmental policy can be a cause of reduced CO_2 emissions.

More formally, causality can be expressed as an (imaginary) intervention in variables: **force** a variable to take on a certain value and describe how the distribution of another variable changes (in the real world). A cause differs from an association: An association is a statement about observing but not influencing. A wet lawn is associated with your neighbor using an umbrella, but it's not a cause. How do we know that? With a (thought) experiment: Water your lawn every day for a year, and see if it changes the probability of your neighbor carrying an umbrella. The reason for this association is, of course, rain, also called a confounder in causal language.

The archetypal statistician avoids causality. It's a historical thing. At least it's my experience, having done a bachelor's and master's in statistics. What I learned about causality in those five years can be summarized in two statements: 1) All confounders must be included in the statistical model as independent variables (good advice!), and 2) correlation does not imply causation (correct but also short-sighted advice). We were taught not to interpret statistical models causally and to view causality as an unattainable goal. We were taught to ignore the elephant in the room.

"Correlation does not imply causation" was like a mantra I heard over and over again.[2] I find it strange, especially considering that statistical modeling is THE research tool of our time. Scientists ask causal questions all the time about treatment effects, policy changes, and so on, and often analysis results are interpreted causally anyways, whether the statisticians like it or not, which is a good argument to learn about causal inference.

The goal of causal inference is to identify and quantify the **causal** effect of a variable on the outcome of interest. Causal inference could be seen as an "add-on" to other mindsets, such as frequentist or Bayesian inference, but also for machine learning. But it would be wrong to see causal inference as just icing on the cake of the other mindsets. It's much more than just adding a new type of method to another mindset, like adding support vector machines to supervised learning. Causal inference challenges the (archetypal) culture of statistical modeling: It forces the modeler to be explicit about causes and effects.

I have seen many models that violated even the simplest rules of causal reasoning. A lack of causal reasoning can completely invalidate analysis, as you saw in the ossification example. It can also make machine learning models vulnerable. Take the Google Flu prediction model as an example. Google Flu predicted flu outbreaks based on the frequency of Google search terms, which was clearly not a causal model. Because you can't cause flu just by searching the wrong things on Google. The flu model failed. For example, it missed the 2009 non-seasonal flu outbreak (Lazer et al. 2014). In the causal mindset, a model generalizes well only if it encodes causal relationships.

The data itself doesn't reveal the causal structures but only associations. Even the simplest causal structures are ambiguous and require the modeler to assume a causal direction. An example: Sunshine duration on a given day might be considered causal for the number of park visitors. In a

---

[2]I have the feeling this is slowly changing though and statistical modeling becomes more accepting of causal inference.

dataset, both variables appear as columns with numbers in them. These variables are highly correlated (association). The causal relationship might be clear to a human but not to the computer. All it can see is the association. *Breaking news: The city has banned visits to the park in an effort to combat the heat wave.*

The modeler makes assumptions about causal directions, the inclusion of confounders, and so on. These assumptions are often not testable and a subjective choice of the modeler. Such assumptions are, therefore, a target of criticism. On the other hand, causal inference makes causal assumptions explicit and encourages discussions. When two modelers have different opinions about a particular causal direction, they have a way of visualizing and discussing the differences.

Visualize Causality With DAGs

Causal inference comes with a tool for visualizing causal relationships: The directed acyclic graphs. A DAG, like the one in Figure 6.2, makes it easy to understand which variable is a cause of another variable. Variables are represented as nodes, and causal directions as arrows.

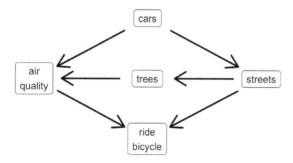

Figure 6.2: To understand the (total) causal effect of streets on air quality, a regression model with air quality as the target should include cars and streets as predictor variables.

What assumptions are made in the DAG in Figure 6.2? Number of cars and number of trees affect air quality (direct causes). The number of streets indirectly affects the air quality through the number of trees (that had to be cut). The number of people that ride bicycles depends on air quality and the number of streets. If the modeler wants to estimate the causal effect of "number of streets" on air quality, then each variable takes on a different role: cars as a confounder, trees as a mediator, and bicycles as a collider (causally affected by both air quality and streets). Each role comes with different implications for dealing with them. You might disagree with the DAG above. Why is there no arrow from cars to bicycles? By making the structures explicit, it's possible for modelers to challenge assumptions.

How does the modeler place the arrows? There are several guides here:

- Good old common sense, such as knowing that park visitors can't control the sun.
- Domain expertise.
- Direction of time: We know that the elevator comes because you pressed the button, not the other way around.
- Causal structure learning: To some extent, we can learn causal structures automatically. But this usually leads to multiple, ambiguous DAGs.
- ...

Pick A Flavor Of Causality

There are many schools, frameworks, and individual models for causal inference. They can differ in notation and approaches (Hernán and Robins 2010). Here is a non-exhaustive overview of causal modeling approaches:

- A lot of causal inference is based on experimental design rather than causal modeling of observational data, such as clinical trials or A/B tests. Causality claims are derived from randomization and intervention.

- Observational data can resemble an experiment, which some call a "natural experiment." When John Snow identified contaminated water as the source of cholera, he had access to data from a natural experiment (two different wells).
- Propensity score matching is a method to estimate the effect of an intervention by matching individuals that are (mostly) identical on a set of background variables.
- Probably the most general and coherent framework for causal inference comes from a statistician, Judea Pearl and covers the do-calculus (Pearl 2012), structural causal models, front- and backdoor criteria, and many other tools for causal inference (Pearl 2009).
- The potential outcomes framework (Holland 1986) is another larger causal school of causality used mainly for studying the causal effects of binary variables.
- Causal discovery or structure identification is a subfield of causal inference that aims to construct DAGs (in parts) from observational data.
- Mediation analysis can be used to examine how causal effects are mediated by other variables.
- There are many individual methods that aim to provide causal modeling. One example is "honest causal forests," which are based on random forests and used to model heterogeneity in treatment effects (Athey and Imbens 2016).
- ...

All approaches have one thing in common: they start from a causal model. This causal model can be very explicit, for example, in the form of a DAG. But it can also be hidden in the assumptions of a method. The final estimate, however, is always something like a statistical estimator or machine learning model. But how do you get from a causal model to a statistical estimator?

A Causal Model Comes Before Estimation

In many cases, a modeler can't perform experiments or trials because they are infeasible, too expensive or too time-consuming. But sometimes observational data is available from which the modeler can try to infer causal effects. However, with observational data, the first casualty is causality – at least from the point of view of non-causalists. But when causal modelers see observational data, they start stretching and warming up their wrists in anticipation of all the DAG-drawing and modeling to come.

Causal modelers say that you can estimate causal effects even for observational data. I am willing to reveal their secret: Causal modelers use high-energy particle accelerators to create black holes. Each black hole contains a parallel universe in which they can study a different what-if scenario. All jokes aside, there is no magic ingredient for estimating causal effects. Causal modeling is mainly a recipe for translating causal models into statistical estimators in the following four steps (Pearl 2009):

1. Formulate causal estimand.
2. Construct causal model.
3. Identify statistical model.
4. Estimate effect.

The first step is to formulate the causal estimand. That means defining the causes and targets that we are interested in. The estimand can be the effect of a treatment on health outcome. It can be the causal influence of supermarket layout on shopping behavior. Or it can be the extent to which climate change affected a certain heat wave.

Once the causal estimand is formulated, the modeler derives a causal model. The causal model can be in the form of DAG and should include all other variables that are relevant to both cause and target.

In the identification step, the modeler translates the causal model into a statistical estimator. Not all causal effects can be estimated with observational data. In particular, if a confounder is missing, the causal effect can't be estimated. Identification can be complicated, but there are at least some simple rules that give first hints for which variables to include and which to exclude:

- Include all confounders and the common causes of both the variable of interest and the outcome. For example, in Figure 6.2, the number of cars confounds the relation between the number of streets and air quality.
- Exclude colliders. The number of bicycles is a collider. Adding colliders to a model opens an unwanted dependence between the cause of study and the target.
- Consider mediators. The number of trees mediates the effect of streets on air quality. Inclusion in the model depends on the goal of the analysis (direct, indirect, or total effect of streets).

The result is an estimator that can be fitted with data. The model can be frequentist or Bayesian, but also a supervised learning model. To estimate the causal effects of other variables, all steps must be repeated. The reason for this is that the identification may lead to a different set of variables for which the model must be adjusted.

Strengths & Limitations

+ Causality is central to modeling the world.

+ Many modelers want their models to be causal. Scientists study causal relationships, and data scientists want to understand the impact on, for example, marketing interventions, etc.

+ Causal models can be more robust, or put another way: Non-causal models break down more easily since they are based on associations.

+ DAGs make causal assumptions explicit. If there is only one takeaway from this chapter, it should be that DAGs are a way of thinking and communicating.

– Many modelers stay away from causal inference for observational data because they say causal models are either not possible or too complicated.

– Confounders are tricky. For a causal interpretation, the modeler has to include all confounders. But the modeler can't prove that all are included. Some might not even be measured.

– There are many schools and approaches to causal inference which can be confusing for newcomers.

– Predictive performance and causality can be in conflict: Using non-causal variables may improve predictive performance but may undermine the causal interpretation of the model.

7 Machine Learning – Learn Algorithms From Data

Premise: The world is best approached through algorithms.

Consequence: Learn algorithms from data to solve tasks.

A machine learner walks along the beach. He sees a bottle in the sand, opens it, and finds a genie who grants him a wish. "I want to understand all machine learning algorithms in the world," he says. The genie nods. "Your wish is granted." The machine learner disappears in a puff of smoke. In his place is a statistician.

It's likely that you've used a machine learning product today. Maybe you have asked your smart assistant to read out your schedule for today, used a navigation app to get from A to B, or checked your mostly spam-free e-mails. In all of these applications, machine learning is used to make the product work: speech recognition, traffic jam prediction, and spam classification are just a few examples of what machine learning can do.

Machine learning is the branch of artificial intelligence that deals with improving at a given task through "experience," which means learning from data. These tasks include clustering, planning, regression and classification, outlier detection, image generation, and text completion. In machine learning, there are not as many constraints on the model as in statistical modeling. Models are algorithms, not statistical hypotheses. Performance is valued over internal validity. For example, a machine learner may use random variables but doesn't have to. The models can be neural networks, DBSCAN, Q-learning, decision trees, density estimators, statistical models and many more. Given this wide range of tasks and model classes: is machine learning a distinct mindset? To answer the question, let's first look at specific mindsets within machine learning. Machine learning is usually divided into supervised, unsupervised and reinforcement learning. Each of these subsets also represents a distinct modeling mindset: They involve a particular view of the world and of the relationship between the models and the world. The supervised learning mindset frames everything as a prediction problem and evaluates models by how well they perform on unseen data. In unsupervised learning, the goal is to find patterns in the data. The reinforcement learning mindset views the model as an actor in a dynamic environment guided by rewards. Deep learning enables learning tasks end-to-end with neural networks.

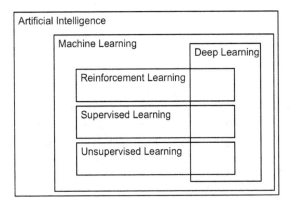

Figure 7.1: Machine learning is a subfield of artificial intelligence. Within machine learning, there is supervised, unsupervised and reinforcement learning. Deep learning overlaps with these 3.

The machine learning mindset may not be as unified and principled as statistical modeling. But all machine learning approaches have a few things in common. Let's take a look at what makes a good machine learning model and how these models relate to the real world.

Put The Computer First

Like all modeling mindsets in this book, machine learning is based on learning models from data. As the name implies, machine learning focuses on the "machine," meaning the computer. Machine learning is about the computer learning to solve tasks such as classification, regression, recommendation, translation, and clustering. How is this different from the work of statisticians, who also rely on computers? The motivation for using a computer differs between an archetypal statistician and an archetypal machine learner. The statistician uses the computer out of convenience and necessity. Modern statistics wouldn't be possible without the computer. Also, their computer is not the starting point but the statistical theory. The computer is only a tool to apply statistical theory to data.[1] The machine learner, in contrast, starts with the computer. The machine learner says, "How to make computers useful?"

Machine learning can be understood as a meta-algorithm: An algorithm that uses data to produce machine learning models that are also algorithms. From a programmer's point of view, machine learning is a paradigm shift: Machine learning means learning an algorithm from data rather than programming the algorithm by hand.[2]

---

[1] There is a field called computational statistics, which is computer-oriented. But we are talking about archetypes of mindsets here. You can think of computational statistics as a statistical mindset that is slightly infused with the machine learning mindset.

[2] I find it difficult to say that the machine learns by itself. Because machine learning also requires programming. You have to implement the learning part and all the glue code to integrate the final model into the product.

Focus On Task Performance

The success of a machine learning model is measured by how well a task was solved. In regression and classification tasks, the machine learner measures the generalization error for new data. Specifically, for a classification model, this could be the accuracy with which the model assigns classes correctly in a new data set or the F1 score. In clustering tasks, success metrics can measure how homogeneous the data points in the clusters are. This external focus is also reflected in the way a lot of machine learning research works: Researchers first invent a new machine learning algorithm and then show that it works by comparing it to other algorithms in benchmark tasks. The reason why the algorithm works well is often only discovered in later scientific publications, if at all.

We can distinguish between external and intrinsic modeling motivation. The motivation and evaluation of a machine learning model are external, based on task performance. It's like judging food based on how it tastes. Statistical modeling is intrinsically motivated. The rationale for constructing the model is important. It's like judging food not only by how it tastes but also by the cooking process: did the chef use the right ingredients? Was the cooking time appropriate, and so on.

Machine Learning As Statistical Learning

Some people refer to machine learning as "statistical learning".[3] Statistical learning is machine learning through the lens of statistics and probability. Many machine learning courses start with this view and talk about conditional probabilities, bias and variance, and probability distributions. Researchers look at machine learning through statistical learning to derive properties of models and algorithms, ultimately

---

[3]Even my favorite machine learning book is called "The Elements of Statistical Learning" (Breiman 2001).

improving our understanding of machine learning. So is machine learning just a rebranding of statistical modeling? Again, it helps to think in mindsets: we can distinguish the mindset of statistical modeling and the language of statistics. Statistical learning means applying the language of statistics to machine learning. But statistical learning doesn't mean that the modeling mindsets are the same. Consider these two approaches:

- A statistician fits a hypothesis-driven logistic regression model and interprets the significance of a coefficient.
- A machine learner tunes and benchmarks ten algorithms and ends up with a random forest to be used for classification.

One could describe both models as conditional probability models and talk about statistical properties. So not only can we describe the models with statistical language, the models even target the same distributional conditional probability. But there is a big difference in the mindset: The statistician starts the analysis with a statistical hypothesis, interprets parameters, and so on. The machine learner evaluates the models differently and has the goal of classification. Even if the machine learner ends up with exactly the same logistic regression model, the interpretation and use in practice would be different.

Strengths & Limitations

+ Task-oriented and, therefore, pragmatic.

+ A job in machine learning potentially pays you lots of money.

+ A computer-oriented mindset in a computer-oriented world
– makes sense to me.

+ Machine learning is predestined for automating tasks and building digital products.

– Not as principled and hypothesis-driven as statistical modeling.

– A confusing amount of approaches and tasks.

– Models that solve tasks well are not necessarily the best for insights. Methods of interpretable machine learning[4] can alleviate this problem.

– Often requires a lot of data and is computationally intensive.

---

[4]https://christophm.github.io/interpretable-ml-book/

8 Supervised Learning – Predict New Data

Premise: The world is best approached by making predictions.

Consequence: Learn predictive models from data and evaluate them with unseen data.

Everything Pete touched became a prediction problem. He could no longer play sports, only bet on the outcome. When he read books, he skipped to the end to check if his predictions were correct. Pete's social life suffered as he was always trying to predict the next words in conversations. His life began to improve only when he discovered supervised learning as an outlet for his obsessions.

It was 2012, and I had just developed a statistical model to predict whether a patient would develop type II diabetes and now it was time to win some money with that model. I uploaded the file with the model predictions to the competition's website, which evaluated the results. Fingers crossed. But then the disappointment: the predictions of my model were terrible.

At the time, I was a master's student in statistics. I modeled diabetes risk using a generalized additive model, a model often used in statistical modeling. More importantly, I approached the problem with a frequentist modeling mindset. I thought a lot about the data-generating process, manually added and removed variables, and evaluated the model based on goodness of fit on the training data. But this approach completely failed me in this prediction competition. I was confused: statistical models can be used for prediction, many models are used in both mindsets, and machine learning is sometimes referred to as statistical learning. This overlap in theory and methods misled me to believe that statistical modeling and supervised learning are mostly the same. But the (archetypal) modeling mindsets are fundamentally different, especially regarding model evaluation. While I didn't win any money in the competition (place 59 out of 145), I did win something more valuable: supervised learning.

In supervised machine learning, everything is a prediction task, typically regression or classification. By "prediction," I mean proposing values for a quantity for which a ground truth exists (at least for the training data). Based on this definition, assigning data points to a cluster is not a prediction because there is no ground truth for the clusters. Prediction can mean assigning a class, a numerical value (regression), a survival time, etc. A modeling mindset that deals only with prediction tasks seems narrow, but surprisingly, many applications can be turned into prediction problems.

- Credit scores: the probability that someone will repay their loan.
- Predictive maintenance: many machines require regular inspection and repair. Time-to-failure can be predicted.
- Demand forecasting: using historical sales data to estimate demand for a product.
- Image classification: how should the image be classified? For example, image classification can be used to detect cancer on CT images.

And the type of data that can be used in predictive models can also be quite diverse: The input to the predictive model, usually called features, can be text, an image, a time series, a DNA sequence, a video or a good old Excel spreadsheet. Once a problem is translated into a prediction problem with data and ground truth, it's time to learn the model.

Learning Is Optimization And Search

A model in supervised learning is essentially just the prediction function.[1] All possible prediction functions live in the hypothesis space. Think of the hypothesis space as a dark forest. A forest with infinitely many functions with different shapes, parameters and forms. Supervised learning algorithms illuminate paths through the forest so that, within these paths, the best prediction function with the lowest loss can be found. The loss measures how close the prediction and ground truth are.[2] While the globally best function might not be within this path, the function might be locally optimal. Supervised learning algorithms put constraints on the functions, which makes the hypothesis space manageable to search. That's where all these different model classes come into play: **decision trees, support vector machines, linear regression models, random forests, boosting, and neural networks** (Hastie et al. 2009). Each machine learning algorithm has its own procedure for searching the hypothesis space. For simplicity, let's say we have only one feature and one prediction target.

- Ordinary least squares: By restricting the prediction function to be linear, the algorithm only has to search for the best multiplier of the feature (the coefficient), which greatly simplifies the search.
- Decision tree algorithms produce prediction functions that look like step functions. The search is simplified to recursively find the best feature values for making a cut.
- Neural networks are universal function approximators that can, in theory, approximate any continuous prediction function (Hornik et al. 1989). For neural networks, the search is simplified to find a good weight configuration.

---

[1]This stands in contrast to statistical modeling, where the model is rich in assumptions and hypotheses about the data.

[2]Another bridge to statistical modeling: both approaches use optimization and any likelihood function (derived from distributions) can also be used as loss functions.

But this search comes with one major problem: overfitting. As long as the model relies only on training data, it's unclear how well the model will predict new, unseen data points. Worse, machine learning models can easily overfit the training data. When the model perfectly memorizes the training data, it will predict the training data perfectly but will likely perform poorly on new data. The opposite of overfitting is underfitting. If the hypothesis space is too constrained, then the model may not be flexible enough to represent the relationship between the input features and the target.

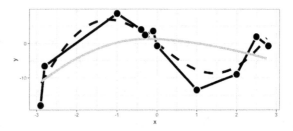

Figure 8.1: The target y depends on the feature x through a function f(x) (dotted line). The observed data (dots) have an additional random error. One model overfits the randomness in the training data (black line), and the other underfits (grey line).

Learning a supervised model means walking a fine line between underfitting and overfitting. The keys to finding that balance are regularization and hyperparameter tuning. Most training algorithms have hyperparameters that steer the flexibility of the model to adapt to data. For decision trees, one such hyperparameter is the depth of the tree: the deeper the tree, the more complex relationships and interactions can be represented by the tree. The tree depth balances underfitting (tree too short) and overfitting (tree too deep). Statistical modelers err on the side of underfitting by putting constraints on the complexity of the model.

Good Models Predict New Data Well

Let's say you want to enter a cooking contest. A jury will evaluate your dishes and insult you live on TV. The jury is the ultimate test of your cooking skills. You have never cooked for these people before, so this is also a test about how well your cooking skills generalize to new data points. But what if your supposed kitchen prowess is overfitting the taste of your family? Let's assume your family loves salt more than anything. The jury would be like: "Did you cook this with seawater?" "What is this? Bread or a salt lick for goats?" In order to avoid bringing shame to your family and name, you decide to validate your skills before this ultimate test. So you cook for people who have never tried your dishes before and adapt your recipes based on their feedback. This way, you can evaluate your skills without having to waste your shot in the contest.

Rigorous evaluation is essential in supervised learning. A typical recommendation is to decide on the evaluation before training the models. Whether a model generalizes well is computed with an out-of-sample evaluation metric. To stay with the cooking example: the evaluation metric could be a rating from 1 to 10. The out-of-sample metric can be different from the loss that was optimized when training the models. For example, you might have optimized your dishes based on how well your family members empty their plates. This metric is computed on so-called test data that wasn't used for training the model, hence "out-of-sample". The TV jury is like test data, because your cooking "algorithm" has never been tested on them. The test data may only be used for the final evaluation. If test data are used for model training or influence choices in any way, the data are "burned" and may not show the true model performance, but will likely be overly optimistic.

Because of this "burning" of the test data, machine learners need a different strategy to train and tune their models. The test data are set aside. To compare models or tune hyperparameters, the machine learner needs unseen data. The trick is to repeat this train/test split within the training data. So the modelers cut off a portion of the training data that can be used to evaluate modeling decisions. This data set is usually referred to as validation data.

Figure 8.2: For honest evaluation, data are usually split into training, validation and test data.

In the simplest version, the data is split once before model training into training, validation and test data. In practice, techniques such as cross-validation are used to split the data multiple times and reuse the data efficiently.

Supervision Enables Automation And Competition

Supervised learning is automatable to a degree that surpasses the other mindsets. Using a well-defined evaluation procedure to target the generalization error, the process of model training can be automated. Supervised learning is essentially an optimization algorithm with a clear goal. Compare that to statistical modeling, such as Bayesian and frequentist inference, where the modelers have to make many assumptions, choose the right distributions, decide on the variables to use in the model, and look at diagnostic plots.

There is an entire subfield of machine learning called AutoML that deals with automating the training pipeline. The pipeline can include feature engineering, model training, hyperparameter optimization, evaluation, etc. Automating the supervised machine learning pipeline is computationally intensive, so there is a lot of research on how to automate everything in a smart way. As a result of this automation capability, there is an entire industry with hundreds of web services and products that automate the training process for the modeler.

Automation can also be problematic. It creates distance between the modelers and the underlying modeling task. Automation can make modelers less aware of the shortcomings of the data. On paper, the model may look very good because the generalization error is small. Under the surface, the model may be garbage because it uses features that are not available at the time of the prediction, or the data are terribly biased, or missing data were not handled correctly, to name just a few possible errors.

The objective evaluation turns supervised learning into a competition of models. It also invites competition between people. Entire websites are dedicated to hosting machine learning competitions where the best modelers can win money. The skills of a modeler are reduced to their ability to optimize for a single metric. A ranking that ignores domain expertise, model interpretability, coding skills, and runtime. The idea of competition has also taken hold of machine learning research itself: scientific progress in machine learning, in some parts, has become a competition of benchmarks.

Mimic Outputs, Not The Process

As we have seen, the mindsets of statistical modeling and supervised learning can be quite different. At their core, the two mindsets involve different ideas of how to model aspects of the world. The following comparison is based on Leo Breiman's famous article "Statistical Modeling: The Two Cultures" (Breiman 2001), which was a great inspiration for this book.

In the context of prediction, nature can be seen as a mechanism that takes features X and produces output Y. This mechanism is unknown, and modelers "fill" the gap with models.

Statistical modelers fill this box with a statistical model. If the modeler is convinced that the model represents the data-generating process well, they can interpret the model and

Figure 8.3: Nature

parameters as parameters of nature. Since nature's true mechanism is unknown and not fully specified by the data, modelers have to make some assumptions.

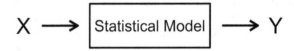

Figure 8.4: Statistical Model

In supervised learning, nature is seen as unknowable, or at least no attempt is made to reverse-engineer the data-generation process. Instead of the intrinsic approach, supervised learning takes an extrinsic approach. The supervised model is supposed to *mimic* the outputs of nature, but it doesn't matter whether the model's inner mechanism is a reasonable substitute for nature's mechanism.

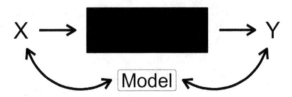

Figure 8.5: Supervised Learning Model

Again, a cooking analogy: Suppose a modeler wants to recreate a dish from a restaurant. A statistical modeler would try to find a plausible recipe, even if the end result is not perfect. The supervised learner would only be interested in the end result; it doesn't matter whether it was exactly the same recipe.

Strengths & Limitations

+ The most straightforward mindset when it comes to making predictions.

+ The choice of loss function allows the model to be adapted quite well to the task at hand.

+ Supervised learning is highly automatable.

+ Supervised learning has a very coherent evaluation approach that I personally find very convincing, though a bit narrow.

− Supervised learning often produces models that are not interpretable but approaches to make them interpretable exist (Molnar 2022).

− Supervised learning is not as hypothesis-driven as statistical modeling.

− Uncertainty quantification is not prioritized in supervised learning, as it is in, for example, Bayesian inference.

− Relying blindly on generalization errors can fail in dumb ways such as using asthma as a predictor of a lower risk of pneumonia (Caruana et al. 2015).

− Machine learning was supposed to free humanity from menial labor. And yet, here we are labeling data for data-hungry supervised learning models.

9 Unsupervised Learning – Find Hidden Patterns

Premise: The world is best approached through identifying patterns.

Consequence: Find hidden patterns in data using clustering, dimensionality reduction and other algorithms.

A group of supervised learners and one unsupervised learner decide to climb a mountain. The trip turns into a race: Who will be the first back to the hut? The unsupervised learner quickly falls behind. After an exhausting day, they return to their hut one by one. To their surprise, the unsupervised learner is already in the hut. Everyone wants to know how the unsupervised learner managed to be so fast. "When you all sprinted off, I took a detour," the unsupervised learner reported, "You won't believe this, but I found a rare type of mushroom. I also divided the area around the hut according to the vegetation. But the best part is that ..." "Wait!" interrupts one of the supervised learners, "How come you did all those things AND were able to climb the mountain faster?" "Mountain? What mountain?"

Tip Top Travel, a travel agency I just made up, offers a wide range of trips, from all-inclusive holidays in Spain to hiking in Norway and weekend city trips to Paris. They have a huge database with the booking history of their customers. And yet, they know surprisingly little about the general patterns in their data: Are there certain types of customers? For example, do customers who travel to Norway also like Sweden? Our imaginary travel company's big data is a dream for unsupervised learners. They might start with a cluster analysis to identify groups of customers with similar travel behaviors.

Together with domain experts, they can try to name the clusters according to the distributions of the features: One cluster could be "families looking for relaxation," and another could be "adventurers."

Find Patterns In The Data Distribution

Unsupervised learning means discovering hidden patterns in data. A dataset suddenly becomes a treasure chest potentially filled with valuable insights. In contrast, for the archetypal supervised learner, patterns are just a means to an end: good predictions.

Unsupervised learning is a machine learning mindset: task-driven, computer-oriented, and externally motivated.

- Task-driven: Unsupervised learning usually solves specific tasks such as clustering, anomaly detection, and association rule mining.
- Computer-oriented: Like its supervised counterpart, unsupervised learning is motivated by the premise of having a computer rather than by the premise of a theory where it's simply convenient to have a computer.
- Externally motivated: While measuring performance is more difficult than in other machine learning mindsets, successfully completing the task is more important than following a particular "recipe" (such as using probability theory).

Unsupervised learning is a less coherent mindset than supervised learning, with its very rigorous evaluation and Zen-like mindset of optimization. "Discovering hidden patterns" is a rather broad modeling goal, and indeed many quite different tasks are covered by this term. But using the language of probability distribution allows us to understand what all these tasks have in common: Unsupervised learning reveals aspects of the distribution of the data:

- Clustering finds modes of the distribution.
- Anomaly detection finds extreme data points of the distribution.
- Association rule learning finds modes in binary feature distributions.
- Dimensionality reduction finds lower-dimensional descriptions of the data.

Why do we need unsupervised learning anyway? Can't we just hire a statistician to estimate the joint distribution and derive all these interesting aspects from that estimate? Unfortunately, estimating the joint distribution is challenging for high-dimensional data, especially for image and text data. Unsupervised learning provides a pragmatic and algorithmic approach.

Unsupervised learning is sometimes called learning without a teacher: there is no ground truth to correct the model. Unsupervised learning is more like, "Here are some data points. Please find something interesting." If the modeler then finds 10 clusters, the modeler can't prove that they are the "correct" clusters. The (lack of) ground truth clearly distinguishes unsupervised learning from supervised learning.

To be more cheerful about unsupervised learning: It's, in many ways, an open mindset. Unsupervised learning means being open to surprises and discovering hidden patterns. The word "pattern" hides a potpourri of meanings: clusters, outliers, feature representations, and association rules. The mindset is also open in the sense that the range of methods is huge, even for a machine learning mindset. For clustering alone, there are so many different approaches. If I had to pick one modeling mindset that is the most inclusive, I would choose unsupervised learning (in terms of methods, not necessarily people). Next to this community of explorers is supervised learning which looks like a bunch of dull optimizers who sit in their offices with fine suits trying to increase sales for Q3.

But full disclosure: unsupervised learning also involves optimization. However, there is more freedom in the optimization objective because there is no ground truth. The same is true for performance metrics and benchmarks: It's part of unsupervised learning to evaluate models, but there's a lot of ambiguity about how to evaluate. For example, in cluster analysis, the model could measure cluster purity, the silhouette score, various indexes, look at elbow plots, and so on. Supervised learning also has a long list of metrics, but at least these usually agree on when to reach their minimum: When the target is perfectly predicted. A luxury that doesn't exist in unsupervised learning.

Unsupervised Learning Has Many Tasks

To get a better understanding of unsupervised learning, let's take a look at typical tasks.

Clustering and Outlier Detection

Clustering and outlier detection are two sides of a coin: Both ask where the mass of the data lies.

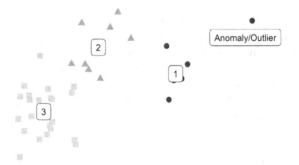

Figure 9.1: 3 clusters and 1 outlier in a 2D feature space.

Clusters are regions in the feature space with a high concentration of data points. In terms of probability, these regions are modes of the data distribution. Outliers are data points in regions with otherwise little or no data. Clusters are usually defined such that all the data points within a cluster are similar in their feature values. There are many different approaches for finding clusters such as hierarchical clustering, k-means, k-medoids, DB-SCAN, PRIM, Gaussian mixture models and self-organizing maps. These methods have different motivations, ranging from statistical to more algorithmic, again showing that unsupervised learning is externally motivated. It isn't particularly important *how* clusters are detected. Different clustering methods may find different clusters.

"Excuse me, how do I get from point A to point B?" "You go down this street and turn right after 10 meters. Then you go another $7 and turn left until red becomes blue!" If features are measured in different scales, such as money and color, it's arbitrary how they should be weighted in clustering or other unsupervised approaches. Supervised machine learning doesn't have this problem. The weighting of features is "supervised" by the relationship between the features and ground truth.

Cybersecurity specialists protect the company from cyber threats: Trade secret theft, malware, digital blackmail, you name it. But there are thousands of employees who leave their daily digital footprint in the network. The specialists use rules to detect some attacks: If someone tries to brute force a password to log into a service, that's a red flag. But what about behaviors that don't follow such simple patterns or new attacks? Fortunately, there is unsupervised learning. Outlier detection, an unsupervised learning task, is concerned with finding extreme data points and helps with cybersecurity. Isolation forests, statistical tests, one-class support vector machines and hidden Markov models – the variety of methods for outlier detection with different underlying motivations shows again that (unsupervised) machine learning is a pragmatic modeling mindset.

Association Rule Learning

I love grocery shopping. Many people hate it, but only because they are unaware of its magnificence: Supermarkets

are incredible places that let you live like royals. Exotic
fruits, spices from all over the world and products that take
months or even years to make, like soy sauce, wine and cheese
– all just a visit to the supermarket away. Sorry I digress,
so let's talk about association rule learning, which is usually
introduced with shopping baskets as an example.

The baskets might look like this: {yeast, flour, salt}, {beer,
chips}, {sandwich, chips}, or {onions, tomatoes, cheese, beer,
chips}. The goal of association rule learning is to identify patterns: Do people who buy flour often buy yeast? Association
rule mining is again a case of describing the data distribution.
An association rule might be {beer} ⇒ {chips} and would
mean that people who buy beer frequently buy chips.

Dimensionality Reduction

Having many features can be a curse. The curse is that the
data density decreases exponentially with each additional
feature. That's a problem regardless of the modeling mindset. Dimensionality reduction can be used to break this curse
or at least to reduce its burden. Not all features contribute
towards the joint distribution equally. Some features may almost have no variance and others may be highly correlated
with other features. A subset of the features may be enough
to represent the data distribution. One way to reduce dimensionality is by removing features based on information-
theoretic measures such as statistical correlation. Another
solution is to map the data into a lower-dimensional space.
This type of dimensionality reduction usually involves a matrix multiplication of the original feature matrix: principal
component analysis (PCA), ICA, non-negative matrix factor-
ization, multidimensional scaling, t-SNE, and so on. If each
data point represents a fruit, features like height, width and
weight might be mapped to a new feature dimension that
represents the volume of the fruit.

Unsupervised learning includes more tasks than just clustering, outlier detection, association rule learning and dimensionality reduction. Others are archetypal analysis, latent

variables, factor analysis, and more. Unsupervised learning is the colorful bird among the modeling mindsets.

Strengths & Limitations

+ Finding hidden patterns in the data that other modeling mindsets (like supervised learning) would miss.

+ The overall mindset is open in terms of tasks, evaluation, and new discoveries.

+ The world is messy. Sometimes modelers have data and a sense that it might be useful, but not yet a specific modeling goal. In this case, unsupervised learning is wonderful as it allows one to just dive into the data without too many assumptions.

+ As a more exploratory mindset, unsupervised learning is a good starting point for analyzing the data with a different mindset.

– A major limitation is the lack of a ground truth, which makes evaluation ambiguous. As a result, there are many methods with often different results (Hastie et al. 2009).

– Lack of ground truth also means there is little guidance on how to weigh the different features for finding clusters, reducing dimensionality and so on.

– Unsupervised learning is a good approach to the curse of dimensionality, but even so, unsupervised learning can suffer greatly from the curse. The more features, the more difficult the interpretation of clusters becomes, for example.

– There is no guarantee that meaningful patterns will be uncovered.

10 Reinforcement Learning – Learn To Interact

Premise: The world is best approached by interacting with it.

Consequence: Model an agent that interacts with its environment guided by rewards.

Two machine learners attend a dinner with a huge buffet. Dumplings are in high demand but unavailable most of the time. The supervised learner tries to predict when the waiters will refill the dumplings. The reinforcement learner leaves and returns with a plate full of dumplings. "How did you get these dumplings?" asks the supervised learner. "First, I tried my luck at the buffet, but of course, the dumplings were gone," explains the reinforcement learner. "Then I thought about my options and decided to talk to a waiter. That decision was rewarded with dumplings!" The supervised learner was stunned, as interacting with the environment never seemed to be an option.

Chess, Go, StarCraft II, and Minecraft: Many people enjoy playing these games. But they have a superhuman competition: computers. All these games require long-term planning and non-obvious decisions. Go has more possible board positions (10^{127}) than there are atoms in the universe (about 10^{78} to 10^{82}). StarCraft II is a complex real-time strategy game that requires planning, resource management and military tactics. Playing these games at superhuman levels was made possible by machine learning. Not through supervised or unsupervised learning, but through reinforcement learning: a modeling mindset that controls an agent acting in an environment.

This agent doesn't sell houses, it doesn't fight Neo, and it doesn't investigate crimes. Reinforcement learning agents play Go (Silver et al. 2016), plan routes, control cooling units (Li et al. 2019), move robotic arms (Gu et al. 2017), steer self-driving cars (Kiran et al. 2021) or guide image segmentation (Wang et al. 2018). An agent in reinforcement learning is an entity that interacts with an environment with the goal of maximizing rewards. This environment can be a video game, a city map, a cooling system, or an assembly line in a factory. Environments may be stochastic or deterministic, partially or fully observable, and have a different complexity. The agent observes (parts of) the environment but also acts in it, thereby changing it. But how does the agent choose its actions? The agent is "motivated" by rewards: Defeating the other players in StarCraft, setting the right temperature in the building, or collecting coins in Super Mario. The "brain" of the agent is the policy. The policy decides what the agent should do next, depending on the situation.

The Model Acts In A Dynamic World

Reinforcement learning is dynamic. When using reinforcement learning to solve a task, the task is viewed as an interaction between a computer (program) and another system or environment. The other mindsets are static in comparison. They work with static snapshots of the world. Interaction between computer and environment isn't part of mindsets such as supervised learning or Bayesianism. In most modeling mindsets, data are usually collected first and then the model is built. In reinforcement learning, the data are generated by the agent's interaction with the environment.[1] The agent chooses which states of the environment to explore and, in turn, which data to generate. The computer runs its own experiments and learns from them. The agent goes through

---

[1]Some data may be collected beforehand. For example, the Alpha Go algorithm was pre-trained by Go moves from human players in a supervised learning fashion (Chen et al. 2018).

a cycle of observing the environment (which might include a reward) and choosing the next action which may influence the environment.

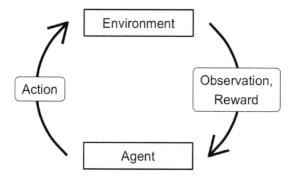

Figure 10.1: An agent observes the environment and chooses an action. The action might influence the environment and produce a reward.

Think about pricing a product. A high price can mean more revenue per sale but fewer customers. A low price can mean more customers but less revenue per sale. The seller wants to find the optimal price that balances demand and revenue. What about supervised learning? The modeler can use historical sales data to train a model to predict the number of sales based on price and other factors like day of the week and promotions. This approach might be suboptimal because it's likely that the price fluctuations did not come through experiments but other factors, such as bonus programs and other dynamic price adaptions. Perhaps the optimal price is higher than any historical price. But supervised learning only learns from observed data; it doesn't explore new options.

Reinforcement learning can deal with this dynamic pricing situation. A change in price changes the environment, which in this case is a tad abstract, as it consists of sales and inventory. Reinforcement learning is a way to conduct experiments with the price. It can handle the trade-off between exploring new prices and exploiting already-learned pricing strategies. This makes reinforcement learning a much more holistic approach that connects interactions.

Reinforcement learning is a typical machine learning mindset. The modeler doesn't care too much about how the agent policy is implemented – the most important thing is that it works. Or, as Ovid said, "Exitus acta probat," the result justifies the deed. The performance of the agent can be measured by adding up the rewards. Just average the rewards over several episodes (an episode is one game or a simulation round) and compare these across models. A reward is an external signal and doesn't rely on model assumptions. But what is a reward anyway, and how does it differ from a ground truth label in supervised learning?

Target Value, Not Sparse and Delayed Rewards

Relaxing is easy, but exercising is hard. Why? There are immediate negative rewards associated with exercise: It's tiring, you have to fit it into your daily routine, and so on. There are also huge positive rewards, such as getting fit and strong, reducing the risk of heart attacks, and prolonging life. These positive rewards occur with a delay of weeks, years or even decades.

Reinforcement learning also deals with delayed rewards, that, in addition, may be sparse. For example, in Tic-tac-toe, there is only a single reward at the end of the game (win or lose). Most actions are without immediate reward and, therefore, without feedback. In Tic-tac-toe, if the agent loses after four moves, how is it supposed to know which moves were the bad ones?

A solution is to assign a value to each state. If there are only a few possible states, as in Tic-tac-toe, a table can fully describe all possible states and their values. If states are continuous or the state space is too large, a function can express the value based on the state. The value function accepts a state as input or possibly a combination of state and action. The output is the respective value.

But what is a value? Simply put, the value tells how good it is for the agent to be in that state. The value is the expected reward for a state or state-action pair. You can think of value as the reward being spread back in time, like jam on a loaf of bread. If you exercise today, it's because you know the value of exercising. You imagine the future reward for your actions today and value the current exercise (aka state) accordingly. Or maybe you don't think about the value at all because working out has become a habit for you. It has become your policy.

Rewards are provided by the environment, but the values are not. The values or the value function have to be learned. One way is to turn it into a supervised learning task! The Go algorithm Alpha Zero, for example, used this trick. Through self-play, Alpha Zero collected a dataset of state-reward pairs. Researchers trained a neural network on this dataset to predict win (+1) or loss (-1) as a function of the game state. Another approach to learning the value function is Monte Carlo estimation: Start from random initial states, follow the current policy of the agent, and accumulate the rewards. Then average the rewards for each state. Unfortunately, Monte Carlo estimation works only for environments with few states.

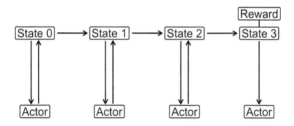

Figure 10.2: Trajectory of a reinforcement learning agent through the state space, with a reward at the end.

Defining the reward can be surprisingly tricky. An agent can behave like an evil genie who takes wishes (aka rewards) quite literally.[2] A good example is CoastRunners, a boat

---

[2]The paper "The surprising creativity of digital evolution" is one of my all-time favorite papers(Lehman et al. 2020). It deals with

racing game. The agent controlled a boat with the goal of winning a boat race, but the score (aka reward) was defined by collecting objects on the race course. The agent learned not to finish the race. Instead, it learned to go around in circles and collect the same reappearing objects over and over again. The greedy agent scored, on average, 20% more points than humans[3].

Learn In Different Ways

For me, this was the most confusing aspect of getting into reinforcement learning: What function(s) are actually learned? In supervised learning, it's clear: the model is a function that maps the features to the label. But there is more than one function to (possibly) learn in reinforcement learning:

- Learn a complete model of the environment. The agent can query such a model to simulate the best action at each time.
- Learn the state value function. If an agent has access to a value function, it can choose actions that maximize the value.
- Learn the action-value function, which takes as input not just the state but state and action.
- Learn the policy of the agent directly.

These approaches are not mutually exclusive but can be combined. Oh, and also, there are many different ways on **how** to learn these functions. And that depends on the dimensionality of the environment and the action space. For example, Tic-tac-toe and Go are pretty similar games. I imagine all the Go players reading this book will object, but hear me out. Two players face off in a fierce turn-based strategy game. The battlefield is a rectangular board, and each player places markers on the grid. The winner is determined by the constellations of the markers.

---

evolutionary algorithms, but it also has more general lessons about how difficult it is to design an optimization goal.

[3] https://openai.com/blog/faulty-reward-functions/

Despite some similarities, the games differ in their complexity for both humans and reinforcement learning. Tic-tac-toe is often used as an example in entry classes and counts as "solved." In contrast, Go has long been dominated by humans. The first super-human Go agent beat[4] the Go champion Lee Sedol in 2016, which was a big media spectacle and a research and engineering feat. The deciding differences between Tic-tac-toe and Go are the size of the action space and state space.

In Tic-tac-toe, there are at most 9 possible actions and on the order of 10^3 possible action-state pairs. The agent can learn to play Tic-tac-toe by using Q-learning, a model-free reinforcement learning approach to learn the value of an action in a given state. Q-learning enumerates the state-action pairs and iteratively updates the values as more and more games are played. In Go, there are $\sim 10^{170}$ possible states. Approaches that enumerate states are futile. To work with these high-dimensional state and action spaces, deep reinforcement learning was used.

Would it be possible to use supervised learning instead? At first glance, rewards seem similar to ground truth in supervised learning. Especially with access to a value function, the policy could be learned with supervised learning, right? Not really. Supervised learning alone is unsuitable for sequential decision-making that requires balancing exploration and exploitation. Imagine modeling a game like Go with a supervised learning mindset: The model would predict the next move based on the current positions on the playing field. The model could be trained with recordings of human games. At best, this supervised approach would mimic human players. But it could never explore novel strategies. Compared to reinforcement learning, supervised learning seems shortsighted and narrow-minded. Supervised learning only considers parts of the problem without connecting actions. Reinforcement learning is a more holistic approach that sequentially connects interactions.

---

[4]https://en.wikipedia.org/wiki/AlphaGo_versus_Lee_Sedol

Combine Reinforcement With Deep Learning

The connection between deep learning and reinforcement learning is rewarding, so let's go deeper here (pun(s) intended). In short: it's a fantastic fusion of mindsets. Reinforcement learning alone struggles with high-dimensional inputs and large state spaces. Go, for example, was too complex for reinforcement learning to solve. Other environments where the states are images or videos are also difficult to model unless you throw deep learning into the mix.

Reinforcement learning is made "deep" by replacing some functions with deep neural networks. For example, the value function or the policy function. Using deep neural networks allows for more complex inputs such as images and helps to focus on end-to-end solutions where the input is the raw state of the game. A successful example of deep reinforcement learning is Alpha Zero which plays Go on a superhuman level. Alpha Zero relies on two deep neural networks: a value network and a policy network. The value network is trained on self-play data to predict the outcome of a game with the Go board as input. The policy network outputs action probabilities based on the Go board (the state). The final policy had some more ingredients, but Alpha Zero proved that using deep learning for some functions in reinforcement learning is beneficial.

Strengths & Limitations

+ Reinforcement learning allows the modeler to model the world in a dynamic way.

+ It's a great approach for planning, playing games, controlling robots, and interacting within systems.

+ Actions of the agent change the environment. In other mindsets, the model is a mere "observer," which is often a naive simplification.

+ Reinforcement learning is proactive. It involves learning by doing, balancing exploration and exploitation, and creating experiments on the fly.

– Reinforcement learning requires an agent. Many modeling tasks don't translate into agent-environment scenarios.

– Often, reinforcement learning, especially deep reinforcement learning, is the wrong approach[5] to a problem.

– Reinforcement learning models can be difficult to train and reproduce because training needs a lot of data, reward design is tricky, and training can be unstable.

– Reinforcement learning models are usually trained in simulation, and performance can degrade when the model interacts with the (physical) world.

– Model-free or model-based? Learn the policy, the value function, or the action-value function? The many modeling choices can be overwhelming.

---

[5] https://www.alexirpan.com/2018/02/14/rl-hard.html

11 Deep Learning - Learn End-To-End Networks

Premise: The world is best approached through (deep) neural networks.

Consequence: Model tasks end-to-end with neural networks and take advantage of emerging properties such as embeddings and transfer learning.

The statistician watched in horror as the deep learner kept adding more and more layers to his model. The model was a monstrosity; she had never seen anything like it. No theory about the data, no guarantees, just millions of parameters.

In 2013, I used a neural network for the first time. A small neural network with two hidden layers. It was disappointing. Training was slow (admittedly on a CPU), and performance was underwhelming. The exercise was part of a machine learning class, and the neural network was just another supervised learning method we learned about, on the same level as decision trees, support vector machines and the k-nearest neighbors algorithm.

Little did I know at the time that the rebirth of "artificial neural networks" was in full swing. Deep neural networks had already crushed the competition in image recognition tasks like the ImageNet image classification challenge (Russakovsky et al. 2015) or a traffic sign recognition challenge (Cireşan et al. 2011). In 2022, the year this text is written, the hype is still going strong or even stronger. The trick seemed to be to give the networks more layers, to make them "deeper."

Mindset Emerges From Neural Networks

Technically, deep learning is "just" neural networks with many layers. A neural network[1] takes input data, which can be images, tabular data, or text data, and produces an output such as a classification score. The atomic units of the network are neurons (and weights), but it's more useful to think of layers as the basic units. The output of each layer serves as the input to the next layer. The input data is transformed multiple times as it travels through the layers of the neural network. In each step, the data undergoes a mathematical transformation parameterized with weights.

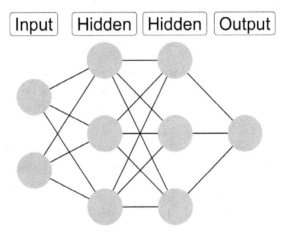

Figure 11.1: A neural network with two input features, two hidden layers with 3 neurons each, and a single output.

Training a neural network means finding weights for the layers that minimize a loss function. Neural networks are usually trained with stochastic gradient descent: Data is fed to the network in batches, and the derivative of the loss is

---

[1]In the early days often called artificial neural networks. Still artificial now, but, who wants to write such long words?

traced back through the network in a process called back-propagation. The weights are changed slightly to improve the loss.

I could have written a similar introduction to support vector machines or random forests, but I wouldn't claim that a new modeling mindset emerges from them. So why say that deep learning is a mindset? I think deep learning is a mindset, but the reasoning is different from the other mindsets. Usually, the mindset implies the models, but for deep learning, the mindset emerges from using neural networks for everything. Not everyone might agree with this view, but I think it's worthwhile to explore deep learning through the lens of a mindset.

Using neural networks exclusively shapes modeling practices:

- Deep learning encourages modeling tasks end-to-end: from raw data to the final outcome. No feature engineering, complex pipelines, etc.
- An emergent property of neural networks is embedding: the learned weights of a neural network store useful information that can be used in feature engineering (like word embeddings) to initialize other neural networks or generate insights.
- Deep learning comes with a high modularity which makes it possible to custom-build a model for a use case.

All these properties make deep learning a coherent framework for modeling. The modeler doesn't have to "leave" neural networks to solve a task. Deep learning has its own center of gravity. In addition, deep learning has a huge community of researchers and practitioners that focus on neural networks, and there is a lot of specialized hardware and software.

I want to distinguish neural networks as a method and deep learning as a mindset with the following story:

Tom and Annie have to classify product reviews as "positive" or "negative." Tom starts with feature engineering: Bag-of-words, which counts the occurrences of each word, removing words like "and," reducing words to word stems, just classic tasks in natural language processing. Since there are too many features, tom uses LASSO (a linear model) for feature selection. Based on this dataset, Tom compares various machine learning models and picks the best-performing one, which happens to be a random forest.

Annie uses neural networks per default. Because of that, she thinks about an end-to-end learning approach, from raw text to classification. She skips feature engineering and stuff because all this happens within the neural network. But 3000 reviews turn out to be too few for the network to learn. Instead of going with Tom's approach, she seeks out a deep learning solution: She takes word embeddings from a neural network that was trained on a larger corpus of text and incorporates it into her neural network. Tom and Annie get a new requirement: Integrate review images into the classification. Tom tries two approaches: the first is to extract features from the images, such as color histograms and edge detectors, which he feeds into different supervised models to predict the outcome. The other approach is to use a convolutional neural network to classify the image. He chooses the latter as it performs better. Then he uses the classification of the neural network as additional input to his random forest. Annie translates the new requirement into an adaption of the current network architecture: She adds the images as additional input to the neural network and adapts the architecture accordingly with the right layers. She later uses the embeddings learned by her model for other tasks, such as clustering reviews. Just when Tom and Annie think they can relax, their demanding boss gives them yet another task: Predict whether a review will be considered helpful by others (for which there is labeled data). Tom trains a new model. Annie adapts the neural network, so it has two outputs: positive/negative and helpful yes/no.

Tom and Annie used similar methods. However, Annie used a deep learning first approach and tried to model everything end-to-end with neural networks. End-to-end learning is made possible by the modularity of neural network layers.

Modularity Allows End-To-End Modeling

Neural networks are composed of layers that can be freely combined as long as input and output dimensions match. Different layers have different purposes:

- Fully connected layer. All neurons in the previous layer are connected to all neurons in the next.
- Convolution layer. Creates regional image-like feature maps for grid-like data such as images or spatial data.
- Embedding layer. Converts categorical data such as words or colors into numeric vectors which relate the categories to each other.
- ...

There is a huge amount of layer types available for various tasks, data types and goals. This arsenal of layer types allows the modeler to customize a neural network for any task. That's why neural networks work with many different data types, from videos to tabular data and sensor data. The modeler can create neural networks with more than one output, or with different types of data inputs, for example, a mix of image and text as in the example.

The glue that holds a neural network together and allows it to still be trained is the gradient. As long as the gradient of the loss can be computed for all layers, modelers can stack layers. Most modern deep learning software packages have auto-gradient abilities and also built-in optimization routines. By wisely picking the loss function, last layer, and evaluation method, the neural network can be used and adapted to any output type, from classification and regression to image segmentation, survival analysis, and deep reinforcement learning. The modelers don't have to leave the world of neural networks. Other algorithms, such as random forests, are not as flexible.

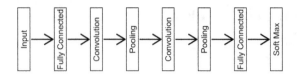

Figure 11.2: Deep learning allows to stack layers.

Properties Emerge From Neural Networks

Curious things happen when a modeler trains a neural network end-to-end: The network might learn to create its own features within the layers, which are stored in the form of activations. This emergent property of neural networks is more than just a fun fact – representation learning gives rise to a style of modeling that is special to deep learning. Let's take a look at convolutional neural networks (CNNs) for image classification. CNNs learn to recognize certain spatial patterns in images. The first layer learns to recognize edges in different directions. The second layer learns to recognize simple patterns. The more layers the data has moved through, the more complex the recognized patterns become. Even concepts like flowers and dog faces can be recognized. See Figure 11.3 (Olah et al. 2017).

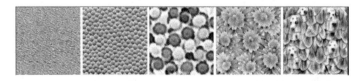

Figure 11.3: Features learned by a convolutional neural network. Features range from edge detectors (left) to more abstract concepts (right). Figure from Olah, et al., "Feature Visualization", Distill, 2017.

Models that are trained on huge amounts of data often have learned reusable feature representations. Deep learning modelers leverage these pre-trained models in various ways:

- Fine-tuning: Retrain the weights of the last layer of a pre-trained network and "freeze" the rest of the weights.
- Embeddings: Use the pre-trained network as a data pre-processing step. Input the data into the pre-trained network, but don't push it all the way through; instead, extract a tensor from a layer between input and output, usually just before the output. Use this feature representation instead of the original features for the next modeling steps.
- Simplify: Keep the pre-trained model, but modify the output. Need a classifier for cat vs. dog? Just take a pre-trained image classification model, but work only with the probability output for cat and dog classes.
- Prompt engineering: Large language models, like GPT-3, can be used for different tasks if given the right prompt. It can then be used for chatbots, text summarization, translation and creative inputs.

Strengths & Limitations

\+ Deep learning works especially well with images, text, and other hierarchical data structures. For these data, deep learning is unchallenged by other mindsets.

\+ Deep neural networks learn features that be reused in different ways.

\+ Deep learning is modular, and networks can be customized for any modeling task. The only other mindset that comes close to this modularity is Bayesian modeling.

\+ There is a large ecosystem of software optimized for neural networks.

– While neural networks win out on image and text data, they lose out on tabular data. For tabular data, tree-based methods such as tree-boosting and random forests dominate the field (Grinsztajn et al. 2022).

– Deep neural networks can be difficult and slow to train.

– Deep learning is crowded. This is a problem for researchers as it's likely that another researcher already works on the same idea.

– Deep learning is data hungry. While statistical modeling is suitable for small data sets, neural networks may need many data points to learn anything meaningful.

12 The T-Shaped Modeler

The shark is coming for the octopus.

Flee. The octopus darts away with a jet of water. But the shark has almost caught up with the octopus.

Ink. In a dark explosion of liquid, the octopus squirts ink into the shark's eyes. A brief window of opportunity for the octopus.

Hide. The octopus begins to squeeze into a tiny notch in the rocky reef. Too slow; the shark sinks its sharp teeth into the octopus' squishy tentacle.

Bite. The octopus counters with its own sharp teeth.

Venom. The octopus' bite is off, and the venom is nothing more than an itch to the shark.

Drop tentacle. The octopus sacrifices the captured tentacle for a chance at survival. Escape now, regrow later. The shark gladly accepts the meal and resumes its pursuit. But where is the octopus?

Camouflage. The octopus has become a part of the reef and lives another day.

The octopus is a cunning creature. But it's also a squishy delicacy to humans, sharks and other predators. To survive, the octopus has many tricks. Famous for their ink and camouflage, they even have a venomous bite and can cover themselves with rocks. Imagine an unsuspecting shark just craving octopus sashimi. Only to come face to face with an octopus paladin in freaking stone armor. The octopus has only a short life of about 1-2 years. I wonder what the earth would look like if octopuses lived as long as humans. Would they build cities and rule the world?

Models learned from data are also squishy and vulnerable. As with the octopus, the best strategy is to pursue multiple strategies when it comes to modeling. Even if models are not attacked by sharks, they are still subject to "evolutionary" pressures: If the model sucks, it might eventually be replaced by something better. A machine learning model might be dropped because it lacks causal reasoning. A frequentist model might cause a product to fail if it is used to make predictions even though the generalization error was never measured. An opportunity could be missed because reinforcement learning was never considered.

Pragmatic Modeling Requires Many Mindsets

I adopted new modeling mindsets to turn projects around. This not only helped the projects but also made me a more pragmatic and effective modeler. By embracing causal inference, my colleague and I were able to improve the (frequentist) statistical model and gain insights into the treatment of axial spondyloarthritis. Switching to supervised learning helped me build better predictive models. Understanding Bayesianism and likelihoodism helped me better understand the frequentist interpretation of probability and recognize its limitations. Unsupervised learning opened my perspective on modeling and being more exploratory when starting new projects. Deep learning unlocked new data types for me (like a side-project to classify x-ray images) and an end-to-end mindset. Reinforcement learning showed me how terribly static most other mindsets are and that models can influence the environment – even if they are not modeled as such.[1]

I've seen experts struggle because they were so narrow-minded in their approach to modeling. If you cling to the

---

[1] Think of predicting traffic jams and showing the predictions to drivers. If drivers now avoid these streets, the predicted traffic jam might never occur: the prediction has changed the outcome, because the model interacts with the environment.

modeling mindset you are an expert in, even when you experience a limitation, you have trapped yourself within the boundaries of the mindset. These boundaries can prohibit you from becoming an effective modeler. Don't get me wrong: you can make a career out of becoming the expert in a particular mindset, especially in academia. As long as you stay in that field, you can excel, like a karateka who has practiced the same kicks, punches and katas thousands of times. But if you put these experts outside their area of expertise, they will get a bloody nose. It's like sending a karateka into an MMA (mixed martial arts) fight. I would put my money on the well-rounded MMA fighter, not the karateka. So if you want to become an extreme expert in one modeling mindset make sure you don't get lured into a street-style modeling task. In a more applied environment, such as working as a data scientist in a company, you don't have the luxury of mindset purity. Your job is to solve a modeling problem. Be like the octopus and adapt your strategies. The world is messy and doesn't like to be confined by the limitations of a singular mindset. Look for non-obvious solutions from other mindsets if you get stuck.

Don't Try To Be An Expert On All Mindsets

It's hard to keep up with new research. Whether it's a causal inference or reinforcement learning, new methods are published daily. There are hundreds of books, online courses and blog posts for each mindset. Even if you stick to established methods, it can take years to gain a deep understanding of a modeling mindset. Realistically, people focus on just a few mindsets. You might start with frequentist statistics but quickly dive deeper into Bayesian statistics. Or you start with deep learning, but you also pick up supervised and unsupervised learning. As you progress in your modeling journey, you absorb some ideas from other mindsets here and there. You might watch a video about reinforcement learning. You read a paper that uses causal inference. You take a class on hypothesis testing (frequentist inference). Yet it remains unfeasible to be an expert in all mindsets.

Become A T-Shaped Modeler

Becoming a T-shaped modeler is the only pragmatic option to knowing many mindsets. The T-shaped modeler embodies a trade-off between being an expert but having some general skills in other mindsets. The "T" symbolizes both breadth and depth. The vertical part symbolizes the mindset(s) that you know in depth. In my case, that would be frequentist statistics and supervised learning. The horizontal part of the T stands for the mindsets that you know a little bit about. My recommendation: Be excellent in a few mindsets, and have working knowledge in others.

Becoming excellent in a few mindsets is "easy." Of course, it's hard work and takes time, but it's a path that many others have taken before you. The path is clear: language, assumptions and ideas remain the same no matter how deep you wander into the mindset. The difficult part is getting comfortable with the other mindsets. Of course, you can take a course on the new mindset. But it can be hard to learn it since language, assumptions, and ideas might be in conflict with the mindsets that you already know well. Expanding your modeling knowledge requires stepping out of your comfort zone and challenging deeply held assumptions that you've spent years, maybe decades, building.

How does the T-shape modeler work? You work on your model in the way you already know deeply. You work in the vertical part of the T. Then you hit a roadblock: your modeling approach can't solve the task at hand because you have reached the vertical end of the T. Each mindset has such limitations. An "I"-shaped modeler can't see the limitations. They will run against the wall and claim the task is the problem: it can't be solved. This is true if the limitations of the current mindset are accepted. A T-shaped modeler, in contrast, knows when the limitations become a cage. A T-shaped modeler looks left and right for answers instead of repeatedly running their head into the wall.

You've reached the end of this book, and I hope you enjoyed the journey. I've poured more than 12 years of experience and many months of work to bring this book to life. I have a small favor to ask: **If you enjoyed reading this book, I would be immensely grateful if you could take a few moments to leave a review on Amazon**[2].

Your honest feedback not only supports my work but also helps other readers in their decision-making process. Sharing your favorite parts of the book or providing constructive criticism can make a significant impact. It doesn't have to be long – even a sentence or two can make a difference.

---

[2]https://www.amazon.com/-/dp/B0BMJH7M9F/#customerReviews

13 Acknowledgments

This book was brought to life by inspiring discussions with Heidi Seibold, Janek Thomas, Malte Schierholz, Florian Molnar, Florian Pfisterer, Timo Freiesleben and Gunnar König.

I would also like to thank all the early readers for their feedback, which made the book more useful and readable: Daniel Kapitan, Luísa Vieira Lucchese, Kevin Yang, Cornelia Gruber, Aaron Wenteler, Tomek Hibner, Ruben Camilo Wißkott, Aaron Wenteler, Ahmed Gdoura, Luis Arias, Ahmed Gdoura, and Tyler Suard. I would also like to give a shout-out to Robert Martin who wrote the first review on Goodreads about an early version of Modeling Mindsets which gave me a boost in confidence when I needed it.

The book cover was designed by vtuber_pro22 (fiverr) and finalized by Heidi Seibold. The octopus on the cover was designed by jeeshiu (fiverr). Proofreading was done by jessieraymond (fiverr). I brainstormed most of the short stories using GPT-3.

More From The Author

If you're looking for a book that will help you make machine learning models explainable, look no further than Interpretable Machine Learning. This book provides a clear and concise explanation of the methods and mathematics behind the most important approaches to making machine learning models interpretable.

Available from leanpub.com and amazon.com.

References

Athey S, Imbens G (2016) Recursive partitioning for heterogeneous causal effects. Proceedings of the National Academy of Sciences 113:7353–7360

Blei DM, Kucukelbir A, Mcauliffe JD (2017) Variational inference: A review for statisticians. Journal of the American Statistical Association 112:859–877

Breiman L (2001) Statistical modeling: The two cultures (with comments and a rejoinder by the author). Statistical science 16:199–231

Caruana R, Lou Y, Gehrke J, et al (2015) Intelligible models for healthcare: Predicting pneumonia risk and hospital 30-day readmission. In: Proceedings of the 21st ACM SIGKDD international conference on knowledge discovery and data mining. pp 1721–1730

Chen T, Wang Z, Li G, Lin L (2018) Recurrent attentional reinforcement learning for multi-label image recognition. In: Proceedings of the AAAI conference on artificial intelligence

Cireşan D, Meier U, Masci J, Schmidhuber J (2011) A committee of neural networks for traffic sign classification. In: The 2011 international joint conference on neural networks. IEEE, pp 1918–1921

Freiesleben T, König G, Molnar C, Tejero-Cantero A (2022) Scientific inference with interpretable machine learning: Analyzing models to learn about real-world phenomena. arXiv preprint arXiv:220605487

Grinsztajn L, Oyallon E, Varoquaux G (2022) Why do tree-based models still outperform deep learning on tabular data? arXiv preprint arXiv:220708815

Gu S, Holly E, Lillicrap T, Levine S (2017) Deep reinforcement learning for robotic manipulation with asynchronous off-policy updates. In: 2017 IEEE international conference on robotics and automation (ICRA). IEEE, pp 3389–3396

Hacking I (1965) Logic of statistical inference

Hastie T, Tibshirani R, Friedman JH, Friedman JH (2009) The elements of statistical learning: Data mining, inference, and prediction. Springer

Head ML, Holman L, Lanfear R, et al (2015) The extent and consequences of p-hacking in science. PLoS biology 13:e1002106

Hernán MA, Robins JM (2010) Causal inference

Holland PW (1986) Statistics and causal inference. Journal of the American Statistical Association 81:945–960

Hornik K, Stinchcombe M, White H (1989) Multilayer feedforward networks are universal approximators. Neural networks 2:359–366

Kao WL, Puddey IB, Boland LL, et al (2001) Alcohol consumption and the risk of type 2 diabetes mellitus: Atherosclerosis risk in communities study. American journal of epidemiology 154:748–757

Kiran BR, Sobh I, Talpaert V, et al (2021) Deep reinforcement learning for autonomous driving: A survey. IEEE Transactions on Intelligent Transportation Systems

Lazer D, Kennedy R, King G, Vespignani A (2014) The parable of google flu: Traps in big data analysis. Science 343:1203–1205

Lehman J, Clune J, Misevic D, et al (2020) The surprising creativity of digital evolution: A collection of anecdotes from the evolutionary computation and artificial life research communities. Artificial life 26:274–306

Li Y, Wen Y, Tao D, Guan K (2019) Transforming cooling optimization for green data center via deep reinforcement learning. IEEE transactions on cybernetics 50:2002–2013

Molnar C (2022) Interpretable machine learning: A guide for making black box models explainable[1], 2nd edn.

Molnar C, Scherer A, Baraliakos X, et al (2018) TNF blockers inhibit spinal radiographic progression in ankylosing spondylitis by reducing disease activity: Results from the

---

[1]https://christophm.github.io/interpretable-ml-book

swiss clinical quality management cohort. Annals of the rheumatic diseases 77:63–69

Olah C, Mordvintsev A, Schubert L (2017) Feature visualization. Distill. https://doi.org/10.23915/distill.00007

Pearl J (2009) Causal inference in statistics: An overview. Statistics surveys 3:96–146

Pearl J (2012) The do-calculus revisited. arXiv preprint arXiv:12104852

Perezgonzalez JD (2015) Fisher, neyman-pearson or NHST? A tutorial for teaching data testing. Frontiers in psychology 223

Richard R (2017) Statistical evidence: A likelihood paradigm. Routledge

Russakovsky O, Deng J, Su H, et al (2015) ImageNet Large Scale Visual Recognition Challenge. International Journal of Computer Vision (IJCV) 115:211–252. https://doi.org/10.1007/s11263-015-0816-y

Silver D, Huang A, Maddison CJ, et al (2016) Mastering the game of go with deep neural networks and tree search. nature 529:484–489

Tiao GC, Box GE (1973) Some comments on "bayes" estimators. The American Statistician 27:12–14

Wang Z, Sarcar S, Liu J, et al (2018) Outline objects using deep reinforcement learning. arXiv preprint arXiv:180404603

Weisberg M (2007) Who is a modeler? The British journal for the philosophy of science 58:207–233

Weisberg M (2012) Simulation and similarity: Using models to understand the world. Oxford University Press

Yang R, Berger JO (1996) A catalog of noninformative priors. Institute of Statistics; Decision Sciences, Duke University Durham, NC, USA